Everyday Idioms

for Reference and Practice

Book One

Ronald E. Feare

Longman

Everyday Idioms for Reference and Practice: Book One

Addison Wesley Longman, 10 Bank Street, White Plains, NY 10606

Editorial director: Joanne Dresner
Acquisitions editor: Allen Ascher
Development editors: Kathy Ossip, Jessica Miller
Senior production editor: Carolyn Viola-John
Production editor: Janice L. Baillie
Text design: Christine Gehring Wolf
Cover design: Curt Belshe
Text art: Len Shalansky

Library of Congress Cataloging-in-Publication Data

Feare, Ronald E.
    Everyday idioms for reference and practice / Ronald E. Feare.
        p.   cm.
    Includes index.
    ISBN 0-201-83408-1 (v. 1)
    1. English language—Textbooks for foreign speakers.   2. English
language—Idioms.   I. Title.
PE1128.F33   1996
428.2'4—dc20   95-53996
                                                                            CIP

ISBN: 0-201-83408-1

12 13 14 15 - CRS - 09 08 07

Contents

Contents

Contents

Preface

Everyday Idioms for Reference and Practice is a two-level series for intermediate through advanced students. The series is designed to make it easier to learn and master common American idioms.

Book One contains more than 700 idiomatic expressions organized thematically into 50 logical, easy-to-access categories including common situations, topics, and functions in English. The idioms within each category share related meaning or purpose. This arrangement makes it easy to successfully find, learn, and remember the idioms.

The over 1,200 idioms in both books were carefully selected from dozens of popular newspapers and magazines, workbooks and dictionaries on idiomatic expressions, as well as idioms samples collected by students at the American Language Institute, San Diego State University. *Book One* includes common and useful idioms that will increase **intermediate** students' ability to comprehend and speak English more fluently.

Unit Format

Each unit opens with a list of idioms with definitions and example sentences that provide clear contexts for usage. Parentheses indicate if a part of the idiom is optional. Many entries also provide additional synonymous, antonymous, or related idioms. If appropriate, grammar and usage notes are included.

Grammar and Usage Notes

Grammar notes are provided when necessary to clearly explain how to use an idiom correctly. For example, some verbal idioms may be used with or without an object:

		OBJECT	
They had to	*wake up*	George	before 6:30.
Ginger usually	*wakes up*		before her parents.

Some verbal idioms are separable; that is, an object may separate the parts of the idiom:

	OBJECT	
I won't *clean up*	the bedroom	if you don't help me.
I won't *clean*	the bedroom	*up* if you don't help me.

Sometimes a verbal idiom *must* be separated by an object:

OBJECT

A cup of coffee **gets**   me   **going** in the morning.

Usage notes provide information about level of formality, social use, and collocations.

Exercises

Exercises in each unit offer opportunities to speak, listen, read, and write. They progress from controlled to open-ended and more difficult.

Exercise A asks students to show they recognize each idiom by completing the missing parts of idioms in single sentences, paragraphs, or dialogues. When a verb is the missing part, the tense or third person singular ending -*s* must be written correctly.

Exercise B asks students to show they understand an idiom by matching a question with its appropriate response. This can be done as an optional listening exercise by covering the questions in the left column and playing the audiocassette, or by the teacher reading the questions aloud.

Exercise C gives students further practice in understanding and using the idioms through pair discussion or writing. Each question uses one or more idioms from the unit.

Exercise D is an open-ended opportunity to practice the idioms through speaking or writing as students role-play, discuss, give an oral presentation, or create a dialogue related to the unit topic.

Review Units

There is a review unit after every ten units. Each review unit provides further practice in using the idioms in multiple-choice exercises, true/false exercises, and crossword puzzles.

It is possible to use a review unit as a pretest to determine how many idioms are really known from the ten preceding units. This may help determine which units should be studied first. If they are not used as pretests, each review unit should be done only after completing the ten units that precede it.

How to Use the Book

This book may be used as a class text, a supplementary text, a self-study text, or as a reference. Though the two *Everyday Idioms* books can be used as a series, it is not necessary to use *Book One* before using *Book Two*. Units can be studied in any order and, by referring to the unit topics, they can be easily used to supplement lessons in speaking or writing. The table of contents lists the categories clearly along with the respective idioms in each unit, making them easily accessible. The index at the back of the book also provides a complete alphabetical listing of the idioms with page number reference. There is a perforated answer key for Exercises A and B and the review units at the back of the book.

Audiocassette

The questions in Exercise B are recorded for every unit. This book can be used with or without the audiocassette. If the audiocassette is used, you may want to do the units in order.

Unit 1
In the Morning

wake up   to awake, to arise from sleep
also: **get up**

GRAMMAR/USAGE NOTES: These idioms can be used with or without an object. With an object, the idioms are separable. (The preface has more explanation on separable and inseparable idioms.) *Get up* literally means "to get out of the bed," which may happen some time after *waking up*.

- Ginger usually *gets up* before her parents, but this morning they had to *wake* her *up*.
- Sometimes after I *wake up*, I lie in bed for a while before I finally *get up*.

crack of dawn   the moment when sunlight is first seen in the morning sky

- During the busy harvest season, farmers get up at the *crack of dawn* and don't stop working until dusk.

go off   to sound, to ring
USAGE NOTE: The subject is usually *alarm* or *buzzer*.

- When the alarm *goes off* in the morning, I jump out of bed immediately.
- Jack was late to work because he didn't hear the buzzer *go off*.

not sleep a wink   to get no sleep (or very little sleep) during the night
USAGE NOTE: The negative term *hardly* can substitute for *not*.

- The Wilsons could*n' t sleep a wink* the first night they spent in their new house.
- The children were so excited about opening presents on Christmas Day that they *hardly slept a wink* on Christmas Eve.

sleep like a log   to sleep very well
also: **sleep like a baby**

- I didn't wake up once last night. I must have *slept like a log*.
- Maria can *sleep like a baby* in almost any place, including airplanes and cars.

take a shower   to shower
related idiom: **take a bath** (to bathe)

- After easy exercise I *take a shower*, but after serious exercise I *take a bath* to relax my muscles.

get ready   to prepare oneself by getting dressed, eating breakfast, and so on

- It takes Linda about an hour to *get ready* for work if she hurries.
- The first thing I do to *get ready* in the morning is to shave.

get someone going   to stimulate into action

> GRAMMAR/USAGE NOTES: This idiom is used when someone is slow to act in the morning. A reflexive pronoun can also be used.
> - There's nothing like a good cup of coffee to *get* me *going* in the morning.
> - Charlie likes to jog every morning to *get himself going.*

start the day off (right)   to begin the day with something good
> - I usually *start the day off* by having some tea and reading the newspaper.
> - Some people like to exercise to *start the day off right.*

sleep in   to stay in bed late in the morning
> - On the weekends, many people like to *sleep in.*
> - Josh chose to *sleep in* after staying up late the night before.

EXERCISES

A. **Fill in each blank with the part of the idiom that is missing.**

1. The Thompsons were so excited about their new baby that they didn't sleep a _____ the night they got back home from the hospital.

2. For some reason the alarm didn't _____ off this morning. I must have forgotten to set it.

3. My Dad and I got up at the _____ of dawn to go fishing.

4. A loud noise made Nellie wake _____ in the middle of the night.

5. Matt is so tired when he gets home that he usually _____ like a log at night.

6. You're all hot and sweaty from working outside. Be sure to _____ a shower before dinner.

7. Every Sunday morning the Jonnas like to sleep _____ until eleven o'clock.

8. A quick jog and cool shower really _____ me going in the morning.

9. Andrew starts the day _____ by taking a shower.

10. How much longer will it take you to get _____ to leave?

B. **Choose the statement in the right column that best responds to each question in the left column. Write the appropriate number in the blank.**

> NOTE: *To do this as a listening exercise, cover up the left column before you start the tape.*

1. How long does it take you to get ready for work?

___ a. I feel lazy too. It must be the rainy weather we're having.

2. Would you like breakfast in bed on your birthday?

___ b. No, I think I'd rather take a bath tonight.

3. Why can't I get myself going this morning?

___ c. If I hurry, I can do it in forty-five minutes.

4. Why are you late for work again today?

___ d. That sounds like a great way to start the day off.

5. Are you going to take a shower before you go to bed?

___ e. I'm sorry. My alarm didn't go off for some reason.

C. Use the idioms in your spoken or written answers to the following questions.

1. When do you usually *wake up* in the morning? Do you always *get up* as soon as you wake up?
2. For what reasons might you *not sleep a wink?* For what reasons might you *sleep like a log?*
3. What do you do to *get ready* in the morning?
4. What do you do in the morning to *get yourself going?*
5. Which would you prefer—getting up at the *crack of dawn*, or *sleeping in?* Why?

D. Using the idioms from this unit, develop a dialogue about your typical morning routine. You may include the following information:

- what time you wake up, and whether you get up immediately;
- whether you use an alarm clock;
- how well you usually sleep;
- whether you take a shower, a bath, or neither;
- how long it takes you to get ready;
- what you do to start the day off right.

Unit 2
In the Evening

go out   to leave home to do an activity (usually in the evening)
- Marco *went out* with his friends very often until he got married.
- Mr. and Mrs. Faulk *go out* for a walk almost every evening.

stay out   to remain away from home at night
opposite meaning: **stay in** (to stay at home)
- On New Year's Eve many people *stay out* late at night.
- There was such a bad storm last night that we decided to *stay in* instead of going out.

stay up   to remain awake at night
related idiom: **wait up**

USAGE NOTE: *Wait up* is often used when someone has to wait for another person, such as a child, to come home at night. *Stay up* can be used for this purpose, but it also has a more general meaning.
- Lisa was too tired to *stay up* for the late-night movie that she had planned to see.
- I can't believe that my parents are going to *wait up* until I get home tonight.

be tired out   to be completely tired (usually at the end of the day)
also: **be tuckered out**

USAGE NOTE: *Be tuckered out* is more informal than *be tired out*.
- I'm sorry that I'*m* too *tired out* to attend the lecture with you tonight.
- After a hard day's work in the yard, Mr. Coulson said, "I'*m tuckered out!*"

fall asleep   to begin sleeping
also: **drop off to sleep, doze off**
- Terence *fell asleep* on the couch while watching a boring movie on TV.
- I like to read in the evening until I *drop off to sleep* around 10:00 P.M.
- One person in the theater audience starting snoring after he *dozed off.*

turn in   to retire, to enter one's bed
also: **go to sleep, go to bed**
- The Fares always *turn in* after watching the eleven o'clock news.
- When do you generally *go to sleep* at night?
- Nancy was so tired that she couldn't wait to *go to bed.*

hit the sack   to sleep

    also: **hit the hay, crash out**

    USAGE NOTE: These idioms are more informal than *turn in*, *go to sleep*, and *go to bed*.

    ■ I'm so tired that the only thing I want to do is take a shower and **hit the sack**.

    ■ Arnold stumbled into the house at midnight and said, "Time to **hit the hay!**"

    ■ Carla didn't mind **crashing out** in her friend's living room during her visit.

bed down   to prepare a temporary place to sleep

    USAGE NOTE: This idiom is usually used for sleeping outdoors in a temporary location.

    ■ The hikers **bedded down** in a different place each night of their weeklong trip.

    ■ The soldiers were told to **bed down** in the barn of an old farmhouse.

after hours   after the normal, or permitted, time

    USAGE NOTE: *After hours* can be used as an adjective when it is hyphenated (-).

    ■ Most large cities have a part of town where people can go **after hours**.

    ■ The popular nightclub stayed open for a special **after-hours** party.

EXERCISES

A.   **Fill in each blank with the part of the idiom that is missing.**

Last Saturday José went _____ with his college roommates. They
1

_____ out at a nightclub until after midnight and then went to a
2

friend's apartment for an after-_____ snack. When José finally
3

_____ the sack at 2:30 A.M., he was so tired _____ that he
4 5

_____ asleep immediately.
6

Before José went to college he lived with his parents, who would always stay

_____ until he came home. One time José was so late that his parents
7

had already _____ in, and all the doors were locked. José had forgotten
8

to take his key and couldn't get into the house. He didn't want to disturb his

parents, so he bedded _____ on the patio until morning.
9

B.   **Choose the statement in the right column that best responds to each question in the left column. Write the appropriate number in the blank.**

    NOTE: *To do this as a listening exercise, cover up the left column before you start the tape.*

1. Are you going to wait up until your son gets home?   ____ a. No, she had to work early in the morning.

2. Are you ready to go to bed yet, Stephanie?   ____ b. No, I'm too tired out. Besides, he's going to stay out quite late.

3. Do you know where your grandfather is?   ____ c. I'd really prefer to stay in tonight.

4. Would you like to go out to see a play later this evening?   ____ d. No, I've still got to brush my teeth.

5. Did Noreen go back to your apartment for an after-hours chat?   ____ e. Yes, he's dozed off on the couch as usual!

C. Use the idioms in your spoken or written answers to the following questions.

1. Do you like to *go out* with friends? Where do you like to go?
2. For what reasons might someone prefer to *stay in* than to *go out?*
3. Have you ever *stayed up* all night? Why?
4. Have you ever *bedded down* outdoors? When and where?
5. Where can you go *after hours* in your town or city?

D. Using the idioms from this unit, develop a dialogue about your typical evening routine. You may include the following information:

- how late you usually stay up in the evening;
- how often you go out;
- what nighttime activities make you tired out;
- when you usually hit the hay;
- how quickly you drop off to sleep.

Unit 3
Around the House

keep house   to do the needed chores around the house
related form: **housekeeper** (noun)
USAGE NOTE: *Housekeeper* refers to a special person who is hired
to keep house.

- In modern societies, husbands and wives share in *keeping house.*
- The Amantes hired a *housekeeper* to do most of the household chores.

clean up   to arrange neatly, to put in order
also: **pick up, tidy up, straighten up**

GRAMMAR/USAGE NOTES: These idioms are separable. They are used for the general
cleaning of homes, rooms, closets, work areas, and so on.

- Mrs. Potter told her son to *clean up* his room before going outside.
- Didn't I tell you to *pick* your things *up* right away?
- The Richards *tidied up* the house before their guests arrived.
- Look at the mess in your closet! *Straighten* it *up* right now.

put back   to return to the proper place
also: **put away**

GRAMMAR/USAGE NOTES: These idioms are separable. They are usually used to refer
to specific items in a house or room.

- You're supposed to *put* the dictionary *back* on the shelf after you've used it.
- We *put away* the Christmas decorations until next year.

fix the meal   to prepare the meal
also: **fix breakfast, fix lunch, fix supper, fix dinner**

- Jack *fixed the meal* Saturday night because his wife was sick.
- Some busy people don't have time to *fix breakfast* in the morning.
- We decided to go to a restaurant instead of *fixing dinner.*

do the dishes   wash the dishes

- Older children are often responsible for *doing the dishes* at night.
- The Nelsons decided to *do the dishes* in the morning because it was so late.

take out   to remove unwanted items from the home

GRAMMAR/USAGE NOTES: This idiom is separable. It is often used with the objects *garbage* and *trash.*

- Could you please *take out* the garbage for me?
- It's time to *take* the trash *out.* It's beginning to smell.

odds and ends   various tasks that need to be done

- This weekend I stayed home and did some *odds and ends* around the house.
- Mrs. Aston drove into town because she had a few *odds and ends* to do.

garage sale   a special sale held in front of a house for the purpose of selling household items that are no longer needed
also: **yard sale**

- I put an ad in the newspaper for the *garage sale* we're having this weekend.
- Some people make money by going to *yard sales*, buying items cheaply, and then reselling them.

clean out   to clean by removing unnecessary items

GRAMMAR/USAGE NOTES: This idiom is separable. It is often used when an enclosed place such as a garage or other storage area needs cleaning after a long period of time.

- The Wilsons *cleaned out* their garage to prepare for a yard sale.
- There are so many old things stored in our closets that we should *clean* them *out* soon.

fix up   to repair, to fix

GRAMMAR/USAGE NOTES: This idiom is separable. It generally refers to making improvements in appearance.

- We needed to *fix up* the front of the house before my parents visited.
- The Garretts like to buy older homes, *fix* them *up*, and then sell them for a profit.

EXERCISES

A.   Fill in each blank with the part of the idiom that is missing.

1. Why don't you _____ out your closet before it gets too full?
2. The children cleaned _____ their room after playing with toys.
3. My roommate moved out of our apartment, so now I have to _____ all the meals myself.
4. The Winthrops always do the _____ right after they eat.
5. Mike, could you _____ out the trash for me?
6. We've hired a maid to come once a week and keep _____ for us.
7. Mr. Cummings enjoys going to garage _____ and looking for bargains.
8. The roof of the house looks in bad condition. Isn't it time to _____ it up?
9. Ms. Owens drove all over town doing several _____ and ends.
10. You forgot to _____ the broom back in the closet after you used it.

B. Choose the statement in the right column that best responds to each question in the left column. Write the appropriate number in the blank.

NOTE: *To do this as a listening exercise, cover up the left column before you start the tape.*

1. Why are you cleaning out the garage today?	____ a. No, they're still on the coffee table.
2. Would you like me to fix lunch for you?	____ b. First I want you to tidy up your room.
3. Have you put away the old photographs we were just looking at?	____ c. Of course I don't like it, but it's important to share the chores.
4. Can I go outside to play, Mom?	____ d. That's OK. You don't know what kind of sandwich I like.
5. Do you like keeping house now that your wife works full-time?	____ e. I can't fix up the shelves if I don't take out the junk first.

C. Use the idioms in your spoken or written answers to the following questions.

1. Do you believe that husbands and wives should share in **keeping house?** Why or why not?
2. Do you **fix the meals** yourself? What do you generally eat?
3. Have you ever gone to a **garage sale?** Have you ever had one yourself? Why do people enjoy going to them?
4. Does your room need to be tidied up? What should you **pick up** or **put away?**
5. What **odds and ends** do you generally do on the weekends?

D. Using the idioms from this unit, tell a classmate about how you accomplish things around the house. You may include the following information:

- whether or not you are good at keeping house;
- what things you often forget to put back in their proper places;
- the last time you cleaned up your room;
- if there is an enclosed area of your home that should be cleaned out;
- if there is anything inside or outside your home that needs to be fixed up.

Unit 4
On the Job

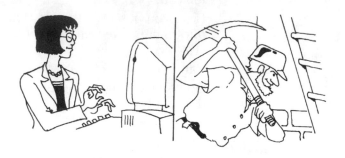

do for a living   to be someone's job

> GRAMMAR/USAGE NOTES: This idiom usually occurs in a direct or indirect question. It is used to ask someone you have met recently about his or her employment.
>
> ■ If you don't mind my asking, what do you do for *a living?*
>
> ■ I didn't ask him what he *did for a living* because I knew he was unemployed.

make a living   to be employed, to earn enough money to survive
also: **earn a living**

> USAGE NOTE: Adjectives such as *decent* and *good* can be used.
>
> ■ My new next-door neighbor *makes a living* as a car mechanic.
>
> ■ It's difficult for single parents to *earn a* decent *living.*

white-collar   having to do with an office environment
related idiom: **blue-collar** (having to do with a nonoffice work environment)

> USAGE NOTE: These adjective forms are used before nouns such as *worker* and *job.*
>
> ■ *White-collar* workers generally earn more money than *blue-collar* workers.
>
> ■ *Blue-collar* jobs such as police work and postal delivery are usually well paying.

put in   to spend time at work

> ■ Some workers choose to *put in* ten hours a day in order to work only four days a week.
>
> ■ Frieda had to *put in* a busy day at the office after she was sick at home for three days.

clock in   to begin work
opposite meaning: **clock out**

> USAGE NOTE: These idioms were first used for jobs where workers' hours were checked with time cards and time clocks. They are still used to refer to the time when someone starts and stops work, even when there is no time clock.
>
> ■ Factory workers are among those who still *clock in* at the beginning of a shift and *clock out* at the end.
>
> ■ Even though I'm expected to *clock in* at 9:00 A.M, I generally get to work around 9:15.

get off (work)   to leave work at the end of the workday

> ■ Deborah *got off work* early because she didn't feel well.
>
> ■ I'll stop by the bank after I *get off* today.

call it a day   to stop working
> also: **call it a night, call it quits**
>
> USAGE NOTE: These idioms can also be used for schoolwork or physical labor.
> - Look, it's already 4:30. Time to **call it a day.**
> - After four hours of studying this evening, I **called it a night.**
> - We've been working in the garden for six hours. It's time to **call it quits.**

close up (shop)   to close a business at the end of a workday
> - I rushed to the bank but I got there just as they were **closing up.**
> - There weren't many customers on the holiday evening, so Mr. Merkur **closed up shop** early.

graveyard shift   an eight-hour work period through the early morning hours
> - Some factory workers work the **graveyard shift**, generally from midnight to 8:00 A.M.
> - Patricia works the **graveyard shift** at the service station so that she can go to school during the day.

EXERCISES

A.   **Fill in each blank with the part of the idiom that is missing.**

FELIX: I'm getting tired. Is it almost time to _____ it a night?
₁

HANS: Are you kidding? We've put _____ only six hours of work.
₂

FELIX: Is that all? I feel like we clocked _____ over eight hours ago!
₃

HANS: You shouldn't complain. Construction work is an excellent way

to make a _____.
₄

FELIX: Maybe, but I think I'd rather have a white-_____ job like my wife.
₅

HANS: What does your wife _____ for a living?
₆

FELIX: She's a store manager. She _____ up shop at 5:00 P.M.
₇

and is home by 5:30 P.M.

HANS: Does she always _____ off work at the same time every day?
₈

FELIX: No, but she never has to work the graveyard _____ like we do!
₉

B.   **Choose the statement in the right column that best responds to each question in the left column. Write the appropriate number in the blank.**

NOTE: *To do this as a listening exercise, cover up the left column before you start the tape.*

1. John, what do you do for a living?	____ a. Of course. Every employee is expected to work a full day.
2. Don't you get tired of working at a blue-collar job?	____ b. No, let's keep working a little longer.
3. Do I have to clock in and out exactly at the right times?	____ c. I'm an account executive at a bank.
4. What are you going to do when you get off work?	____ d. No. For me it's better than being stuck in an office.
5. Are you ready to call it quits?	____ e. I thought I'd go to the store to get some groceries.

11

C.   **Use the idioms in your spoken or written answers to the following questions.**

1. If you work now, what do you *do for a living?* Do you enjoy it?
2. If you don't work now, how would you like to *make a living* in the future?
3. Why are *white-collar* jobs generally considered more desirable than *blue-collar* jobs?
4. How many hours per week do workers in your country *put in?* Do any workers *put in* a four-day workweek?
5. What are the advantages and disadvantages of working the *graveyard shift?*

D.   **Using the idioms from this unit, develop a presentation describing the job that someone you know has. You may include the following information:**

- what the person does for a living;
- if he or she earns a good living at this job;
- if it is a white-collar or blue-collar job;
- how many hours the person puts in each day;
- when he or she gets off work.

Unit 5
Vacation Time

have off   to have time when one doesn't have to work at one's job or attend school
also: **take off, be off**

GRAMMAR/USAGE NOTES: These idioms are separable, and the object is usually placed after the verb. They are used with time expressions such as *days, weeks, months,* and *years.*

■ Next week would be a good time to go fishing, since I **have** a few days **off.**

■ Can you **take off** a couple of weeks for a Caribbean island vacation?

■ I'm sorry, but Mr. Watanabe **is off** until next month. Would you like to leave a message?

on leave   on holiday from military service, not on active duty

■ Sergeant Anders went **on leave** to attend his sister's wedding.

■ The naval officers were assigned to be **on leave** in Singapore for a week.

go away   to travel
also: **get away**

■ Mr. Walters has to **go away** often to run his international import/export business.

■ Are you going to be able to **get away** this holiday weekend?

see off   to say farewell (often by accompanying someone to an airport, station, etc.)
GRAMMAR NOTE: This idiom is separable.

■ Everyone was quite sad the day we **saw** my parents **off** at the airport.

■ The whole family went to the cruise terminal to **see off** the newlyweds.

take in   to experience, to enjoy by viewing
also: **soak in**

USAGE NOTE: These idioms are most often used with words like *attractions* and *sights.*

■ The amusement park was so crowded that we couldn't **take in** all the attractions.

■ We saved a whole week of our trip to **soak in** the sights and sounds of Paris.

check in   to register at a hotel
also: **check into**
related form: **check-in** (noun or adjective)

■ The group leader told the tourists that it would be two hours before they could **check in.**

■ The elderly couple asked if they could **check into** the hotel before noon.

■ There was no line at **check-in,** so Holly got to her room quickly.

■ Could you please tell me your **check-in** time?

13

check out (of)   to end one's stay at a hotel
    related form: **check-out** (noun or adjective)
- The Zorbas got up early and *checked out of* the hotel by 6:00 A.M.
- Beatrice stood in the long line at *check-out* while we waited in the lobby.
- Ted called the hotel operator to inquire about the *check-out* time.

book up   to reserve all rooms
    GRAMMAR NOTE: This idiom is often used in the passive form.
- The organizers of the computer convention *booked up* several hotels and conference facilities.
- I'm sorry, we don't have any more rooms available. The hotel *is* fully *booked up.*

get back   to return home from vacation
    USAGE NOTE: This idiom is also used for returning from work, recreation, errands, and so on.
- The salesperson wanted to know when the boss would *get back* from vacation.
- Our trip was so terrible that I couldn't wait to *get back.*
- Jerry went hunting early in the morning and didn't *get back* until dark.

EXERCISES

A.   Fill in each blank with the part of the idiom that is missing.

1. Do you have any time _____ next month for a camping trip in the mountains?

2. Kathy didn't go to work so that she could _____ her aunt and uncle off at the train station.

3. Did you ask the hotel clerk what time we can _____ in?

4. Local businesses are very happy when sailors go on _____ and spend money freely.

5. We should make our reservations soon or the hotel might be _____ up.

6. When do you expect to _____ back from your trip?

7. This year the Farrs are too busy to go _____ during the holidays.

8. The manager allowed us to check _____ of the hotel two hours late.

9. I love to go for long walks in foreign cities and just _____ in the sights.

B.   Choose the statement in the right column that best responds to each question in the left column. Write the appropriate number in the blank.

NOTE: *To do this as a listening exercise, cover up the left column before you start the tape.*

1. Would you like me to see you off at the airport?

2. Sergeant, are you on leave next month?

3. Hasn't it been a long time since you've had some time off?

4. Were you able to enjoy all the attractions at Disney World?

5. Have you checked out of the hotel yet?

_____ a. I'm going down to the check-out desk right now.

_____ b. Yes, I guess it's been two years since I went away somewhere.

_____ c. Please don't. I hate having to say goodbye.

_____ d. No, a week wasn't enough to take in all the activities.

_____ e. Unfortunately, I don't have any leave until the end of the month.

C.   **Use the idioms in your spoken or written answers to the following questions.**

1. When was the last time that you *got away?* Where did you go and what did you do?

2. When is the next time that you'll *have* a day or two *off* from work or school? Do you know what you will do?

3. Why might someone want to *check into* a hotel early? To *check out* late?

4. What things do you have to do when you *get back* from a long trip?

5. Why might a hotel *be* completely *booked up?* In such a case, what would you do?

D.   **Using the idioms from this unit, tell a classmate about your last vacation. You may include the following information:**

- how much time you had off;
- where you went away to;
- if anyone saw you off;
- what attractions you took in;
- when you got back.

Unit 6
Resting and Relaxing

take a nap   to sleep (usually for a short time)
> also: **take a snooze**

- Every afternoon old Mr. Jones *takes a nap* on his porch for an hour.
- I lay down on the couch and *took a* quick *snooze* in the afternoon.

take a break   to rest by stopping work or play
> also: **take a breather**

- We've been working hard on this spreadsheet for over three hours. It's time to *take a break.*
- The hikers *took a breather* during a very steep portion of the trail.

take it easy   to relax, not to work hard
> USAGE NOTE: This idiom may be used when someone is upset and should relax.

- There's no reason to work so hard. *Take it easy!*
- Why is Eduardo so angry at Elaine? He should *take it easy.*

have free time   to have little or no work to do, to have extra time
> also: **have time on one's hands, have time to kill**

- Whenever Mr. Ness *has free time*, he goes camping in the mountains.
- Amy's job is so easy that she *has* lots of *time on her hands* to read.
- Because we *had time to kill* in San Diego, we saw a few more sights.

pass the time   to spend time (usually relaxing)
> also: **while away**
> USAGE NOTE: This idiom is followed by an expression of time, such as *the hours, the days,* and so on.

- Our flight was delayed on departure, so we *passed the time* playing cards.
- On the small island of Tahiti, we had nothing to do but *while away* the hours at the beach.

daydream   to think about something not related to what is happening at that moment
> GRAMMAR/USAGE NOTES: This idiom is used when a person is not aware of what is happening around him or her because the person is thinking about other matters. It can also be used as a noun.

- Sandra sat at her desk and *daydreamed* about being with her boyfriend.
- It would be dangerous for an airline pilot to have a *daydream* while flying.

loosen up   to become more relaxed, to become informal
also: **let one's hair down**

- This vacation is just the right way for me to *loosen up* and enjoy myself.
- Alana is serious at the office, but at parties she likes to *let her hair down*.

EXERCISES

A.   **Fill in each blank with the part of the idiom that is missing.**

1. It's too hot to keep working in the sun now. Let's _____ a break.
2. Why are you always so serious? You should try to _____ up a little.
3. When our family had its annual reunion, we _____ the time by talking and playing together.
4. One of the students looked like he was _____ as he looked out the window of the classroom.
5. Do you have any _____ time to help me with my research project?
6. Nancy got very little sleep last night so she's _____ a nap on the couch.
7. Why are you walking up the hill so quickly? Take it _____!

B.   **Choose the statement in the right column that best responds to each question in the left column. Write the appropriate number in the blank.**

NOTE: *To do this as a listening exercise, cover up the left column before you start the tape.*

1. Isn't this vacation the perfect way for us to loosen up?
2. Were you just daydreaming?
3. Is your new job still quite difficult for you?
4. Are you going to work this weekend or just take it easy?
5. When will you be ready to take a break from this yardwork?

____ a. No. It's become so easy that I just while away the hours.
____ b. You're right. We certainly deserve this break from work.
____ c. Let's take a short breather right now.
____ d. Yes, I was thinking about our last trip to the desert.
____ e. I just want to relax and watch football games on TV.

C.   **Use the idioms in your spoken or written answers to the following questions.**

1. Do you like to *take naps?* Why or why not?
2. Do you *have* a lot *of free time* in your life, or are you always very busy? Why?
3. If you were staying in the mountains without a television or telephone, how would you *pass the time?*
4. Do you ever have *daydreams?* If so, what do you like to daydream about?
5. What do people do at an office party to *loosen up?*

D.   **Using the idioms from this unit, tell a classmate about a typical workday in your life. You may include the following information:**

- whether you work hard or take it easy;
- how often you take a break;
- whether you daydream while working;
- whether you have any free time after you finish work.

Unit 7
An Active Lifestyle

early bird   someone who likes to rise early in the morning
- I've always been an *early bird.* I rarely get up after six o'clock in the morning.
- Jake's new job forces him to be an *early bird.* He has to start work at 5:00 A.M.

night owl   someone who likes to stay awake late at night
- It's easy for Laura to study until three in the morning. She's always been a *night owl.*
- Scientists believe that body chemistry may determine whether someone is more likely to be an early bird or a *night owl.*

night on the town   an evening of dining and entertainment
USAGE NOTE: This idiom is often used with the verb *spend.*
- Mr. Frederick impressed his fiancée with an expensive *night on the town.*
- Matt and Tina spent a *night on the town* with their guests from Europe.

live (life) in the fast lane   to lead a very active social life
related form: **life in the fast lane** (noun)
- Jet-setters are rich people who travel around the world living *life in the fast lane.*
- How's *life in the fast lane*, Van? You're gone so often I hardly see you anymore!

live it up   to enjoy life by spending money freely
also: **do it up (right)**
GRAMMAR NOTE: The pronoun *it* cannot be changed or removed.
- The Pierces go to Las Vegas once a year and *live it up* in the best hotel suite available.
- We shouldn't worry about how much we spend on our vacation. We should *do it up right.*

have a ball   to enjoy oneself greatly, to have pleasure
also: **have a good time**
- Thanks so much for inviting us to the party. We really *had a ball.*
- Matt didn't expect to *have a good time* at the picnic, but he actually did.

party animal   someone who likes to have fun often
- Up late again last night? This is the third day, you *party animal!*
- Dave had become such a *party animal* that he failed two classes.

throw a party   to invite guests to a party

USAGE NOTE: Words such as *farewell*, *retirement*, and *graduation* can precede *party*.

- Are you free next Saturday evening? I'm ***throwing a party*** and I'd like you to come.
- The employees ***threw a*** farewell ***party*** before their supervisor left for another job.

get out (and about)   to leave home for a social activity

USAGE NOTE: This idiom is usually used when someone doesn't leave home often enough due to overwork, injury, or old age.

- Since our child was born, my wife and I ***get out*** much less often.
- You should try to ***get out and about*** more now that you've recovered from the accident.
- Mrs. Carlson tends to stay home and watch TV. She should ***get out and about*** more often.

EXERCISES

A.   **Fill in each blank with the part of the idiom that is missing.**

FAYE: Have you heard that Larry is throwing a _____ this weekend?
                                                              1

ANN: Another one so soon? What a party _____ he is!
                                                        2

FAYE: He certainly lives life in the fast _____. So do you want to go?
                                                          3

ANN: I'd like to. We _____ a ball at the last party.
                                4

FAYE: We sure did. Larry and his friends provided great food and there was a live

band. They sure know how to live it _____.
                                                    5

ANN: Thanks to the money that Larry's rich parents give him! What night is the party?

FAYE: Saturday. Can you go?

ANN: Oh, that's when Andy invited me out for a night on the _____.
                                                                      6

FAYE: Andy? I thought his leg was broken.

ANN: It's almost fully healed, so he's able to _____ out and about now.
                                                          7

FAYE: Wouldn't he want to go to the party too?

ANN: I don't think so. He's not much of a night _____, you know. In fact,
                                                          8

he's one of the few _____ birds I know!
                            9

B. Choose the statement in the right column that best responds to each question in the left column. Write the appropriate number in the blank.

NOTE: *To do this as a listening exercise, cover up the left column before you start the tape.*

1. How much money did you spend on your trip?

2. Would you like to go out for a night on the town if I pay for everything?

3. Are you really throwing a party this weekend?

4. Would you like to go out to a nightclub again tonight?

5. Why doesn't old Mr. Olsen get out and about more?

____ a. Great. If you're paying, we can really have a ball!

____ b. I'm not sure, but I do know that we lived it up.

____ c. No thanks. I'm not the party animal that you are!

____ d. Yes, I am, and of course you're invited.

____ e. It's hard for him to have a good time since his wife died.

C. Use the idioms in your spoken or written answers to the following questions.

1. Are you an *early bird*, a *night owl*, or neither? Explain.
2. When was the last time that you *threw a party?* Who did you invite?
3. Describe the lifestyle of a *party animal.* Are you (or have you ever been) a *party animal?* Why or why not?
4. If you were rich, how would you spend a *night on the town?*
5. Why is it important for older people to *get out and about?*

D. Using the idioms from this unit, develop a dialogue about your present lifestyle. You may include the following information:

- whether you are an early bird or a night owl;
- whether you like to throw parties;
- how often you go out for a night on the town;
- whether you are careful with your money or you live it up.

Unit 8
Transportation

get around   to move, to travel
also: **get about**
USAGE NOTE: These idioms refer to one's daily means of transportation.
- How do you *get around* if you haven't bought a car yet?
- Since her operation, eighty-year-old Mrs. Jackson has used a wheelchair to *get about*.

get out of   to exit, to leave
also: **get off**
GRAMMAR/USAGE NOTES: You *get out of* a car or truck, but you *get off* a bus, train, subway, motorcycle, or bicycle. *Get out of* must be followed by a noun phrase; *get off* sometimes is followed by a noun phrase, but at other times it isn't.
- Mr. Nguyen *got out of* the taxi as soon as it stopped at the curb.
- Linda wasn't paying attention, so she *got off* the subway at the wrong station.
- Mr. Wells's daughter was scared while riding on her dad's motorcycle, so she asked to *get off*.

get in(to)   to enter
also: **hop in(to), get on, hop on**
GRAMMAR/USAGE NOTES: You *get in(to)* or *hop in(to)* a car or truck; you *get on* or *hop on* a bus, train, subway, motorcycle, or bicycle. When *into* is used, a noun phrase must follow. When *in* is used, a noun phrase may or may not follow.
- Mr. Olson *got into* the car to start the engine. His wife *got in* a short time later.
- I'd be glad to give you a ride to the store. *Hop in!*
- The high school students *got on* the bus when it arrived at the corner.

ride shotgun   to ride in the front passenger's seat
- Jake's brother *rode shotgun* for the entire trip across the United States.
- If you'd like to drive now, I don't mind *riding shotgun.*

take a spin   to drive for pleasure, usually for a short time
also: **go for a spin, go for a ride**
- Would you like to *take a spin* before you decide whether to buy this truck?
- We *went for a spin* around the block in Helen's new car.
- It was a beautiful day to *go for a ride* in the country.

on someone's tail   following too closely behind
> related form: **tailgate** (verb)
> - I'd better change lanes. There's a large truck right *on my tail.*
> - The sports car was *tailgating* the car ahead when the accident occurred.

make good time   to travel efficiently (without wasting time)
> - We *made good time* on our cross-country drive, which took only six days.
> - We arrived at our relative's house an hour early because we'd *made good time.*

fill up   to fill one's vehicle with gas
> also: **gas up**
> GRAMMAR NOTE: These idioms may or may not be used with noun phrases. When noun phrases are used, the idioms are separable.
> - Look, we're low on gas. We'll have to stop at the next gas station to *fill up.*
> - Did you *gas* the car *up* on your way home?

gas-guzzler   a vehicle that consumes too much gas
> - Sascha replaced her old *gas-guzzler* with a modern economy car.
> - During the 1960s and 1970s, U.S. auto companies produced large *gas-guzzlers.*

take off   to depart from an airport runway
> opposite meaning: **touch down**
> related form: **take-off** (noun)
> - Several airplanes were waiting to *take off* because of the busy holiday weekend.
> - The plane *touched down* gently on the runway and taxied to the terminal.
> - On *take-off* the pilot banked the plane to the left and headed west toward Tokyo.

EXERCISES

A.   **Fill in each blank with the part of the idiom that is missing.**

1. Would you like to _____ a spin on my new motorcycle?

2. I'm tired of riding _____. Let me drive now, OK?

3. Mr. Simpson always opens the door for his wife before she _____ out of the car.

4. Since she broke her leg, Prenprapa has to get _____ on crutches.

5. It took us only five hours to go 300 miles. We really _____ good time.

6. We parked our car near the airport runway and watched the airplanes _____ off.

7. Sema moved into the slow lane because there was a fast car on her _____.

8. I can take you to the market on my way to the mall. Get _____.

9. Don't forget to fill the gas tank _____. It's almost empty.

10. As oil prices rise, it becomes less and less economical to own a gas-_____.

B. Choose the statement in the right column that best responds to each question in the left column. Write the appropriate number in the blank.

NOTE: *To do this as a listening exercise, cover up the left column before you start the tape.*

1. Did you help your grandmother get out of the car?

2. Shouldn't we stop at the service station and fill up?

3. Why don't you get in the car?

4. When you were in London, how did you get about?

5. Why are you tailgating the car in front of you?

____ a. We used the bus and subway systems.

____ b. I can't. The door is locked.

____ c. I offered, but she didn't need my assistance.

____ d. No, we still have plenty of gas.

____ e. I want the driver to move to the right so that I can pass.

C. Use the idioms in your spoken or written answers to the following questions.

1. Do any people in your country own *gas-guzzlers?* Why would someone want one?

2. Have you ever *gone for a spin* on a motorcycle? Did you feel safe? Why or why not?

3. Do you look outside the window while your plane is *taking off?* Why or why not?

4. Do you prefer to drive yourself or to *ride shotgun?* What are the advantages of each?

5. Explain how you can *make good time* on a long car trip.

D. Using the idioms from this unit, develop a presentation describing transportation in your country. You may include the following information:

- how most people get around;
- how you usually get about;
- on which side of a vehicle the driver gets in and out;
- what kinds of vehicles are gas-guzzlers;
- when and where people in your city like to go for a spin.

Unit 9
Commuting

take off (to work)   to depart immediately, to leave quickly
   also: **rush off**
- I'm going to be late for work if I don't *take off* right now.
- Before Leroy could ask another question, Brenda *rushed off* to work.

buckle up   to fasten one's seatbelt
- Some drivers of cars with airbags think it's unnecessary to *buckle up* too.
- Signs on the highways remind people that *buckling up* can save lives.

drop off   to deliver someone to a place
   opposite meaning: **pick up** (to take someone from a place)
   GRAMMAR NOTE: This idiom is separable, and the object is usually placed after the verb.
- My son Elijah asked me to *drop* him *off* at school on my way to work because it was raining.
- He also wanted me to *pick* him and his friend *up* if it was still raining after school.

give a lift   to transport someone in one's vehicle
   also: **give a ride**
   GRAMMAR NOTE: These idioms must be separated by a noun or pronoun after the verb.
- The young woman hitchhiking on the highway looked nice, so Vince *gave* her *a lift*.
- Could you *give* me *a ride* to the airport next Wednesday? I'd appreciate it.

on one's way   in the direction that one is going
   opposite meaning: **out of one's way** (not in the direction that one is going)
- Since the post office was *on my way* to the supermarket, I stopped there for some stamps.
- It's no problem for William to give you a ride there. It's not *out of his way*.

rush hour   the busiest commuting time (usually 6–9 A.M. and 4–7 P.M.)
   GRAMMAR NOTE: This compound noun can be hyphenated (–) to make an adjective form preceding the noun *traffic*.
- It takes Philip three hours to commute to work during *rush hour*.
- *Rush-hour* traffic is generally lighter on Friday afternoons.

share a ride   to commute with one or more persons in the same car
also: **rideshare**
related form: **ridesharing** (noun)

- Some companies provide special benefits when employees agree to *share a ride* to work.
- The university maintains a list of people who want to *rideshare* to school.
- *Ridesharing* is one of the best ways to reduce air pollution caused by automobiles.

carpool lane   a special lane on city highways for cars with at least two people inside
related form: **carpool** (verb)

- You will have to pay a large fine if you drive in the *carpool lane* without at least one other passenger.
- The office workers *carpooled* to avoid the heavy traffic in the other highway lanes.

double-park   to park in the street illegally next to a car that is parked legally along the curb
related form: **double-parking** (noun)
USAGE NOTE: This idiom is used to describe what happens when there are no available parking spaces along the curb of a street.

- Frank *double-parked* in front of the bakery in order to pick up the cake.
- *Double-parking* is unavoidable in some American cities where it is too crowded to park legally.

EXERCISES

A.   **Fill in each blank with the part of the idiom that is missing.**

1. Gene was late to work because he got stuck in rush-_____ traffic.

2. If you could _____ Camille off at the music store, I'll pick her up when her lessons are done.

3. The police officer ticketed a driver in the _____ lane who was not carrying a passenger.

4. I can take you to soccer practice because it's on my _____ to the store.

5. Statistics prove that many lives are saved when drivers and passengers _____ up.

6. If I don't take _____ for work right now, I'll be late again.

7. Jane's co-worker _____ her a lift to the garage where her car was being repaired.

8. If you move near our neighborhood, we can _____ a ride to work together.

9. Elijah couldn't find a parking space, so he _____-parked and quickly ran into the dry cleaning store to get his coat.

B. Choose the statement in the right column that best responds to each question in the left column. Write the appropriate number in the blank.

NOTE: *To do this as a listening exercise, cover up the left column before you start the tape.*

1. Would you mind giving me a ride to the shopping mall?

2. Why are you ridesharing with other employees at your job?

3. Isn't it illegal to double-park here in front of the store?

4. Did you drive through Los Angeles before rush hour started?

5. Would you like me to drop you off in front of the theater?

____ a. Yes, we were well north of there by 5:00 A.M.

____ b. I'm sorry, but it's really out of my way.

____ c. That would be good. And could you pick us up around 5:00 P.M.?

____ d. So we can use the carpool lane to get to work every day.

____ e. But there's nowhere else to park!

C. Use the idioms in your spoken or written answers to the following questions.

1. Would you *give someone* who was hitchhiking *a lift?* Why or why not?

2. In the United States, *ridesharing* is not yet popular, and most cars on the highways contain only one person. Can you think of some reasons why this is true? What is the situation in your country?

3. In many states in the United States, the law requires that you have to *buckle up.* Do you think that this is a necessary law? Why or why not?

4. Are there *carpool lanes* in your country? If not, should there be?

5. Do you often *rush off* to work or school? Why or why not?

D. Using the idioms from this unit, tell a classmate about your commute to work or school. You may include the following information:

- at what time you take off for work or school;
- whether your commute is affected by rush hour;
- who gives you a lift when you need one;
- what stores are on your way to work or school;
- whether you've ever used a carpool lane.

Unit 10
The Weather

cool down   to become cooler in temperature
also: **cool off**

- During the summer everyone is glad when evening comes and the weather *cools down.*
- The weather reporter says that it should *cool off* by the weekend.

heat up   to make or become warmer in temperature

GRAMMAR/USAGE NOTES: Besides weather, this idiom is used for room temperature, cooking, and such. When an object is used, the idiom is separable.

- We should open all the windows tomorrow morning before the weather *heats up.*
- The room *heated up* quickly with thirty-five people inside.
- Could you *heat* some water *up* for the coffee?

rain cats and dogs   to rain very hard
also: **beat down**

GRAMMAR/USAGE NOTES: The subject pronoun *it* must be used with *rain cats and dogs.* The idiom *beat down* can also be used to refer to intense heat from sun rays.

- Look outside! It's *raining cats and dogs* right now.
- The rain was *beating down* on the roof so hard that it sounded like hail.
- The desert sun *beat down* on the lost hikers, making them thirsty and sweaty.

run off   to flow from a high place to a lower place
related form: **runoff** (noun)

USAGE NOTE: This idiom is used to refer to excessive amounts of rainwater.

- It rained so long and hard that water *ran off* the hills and flooded many communities.
- The source of all rivers, such as the Mississippi, is *runoff* from mountain streams.

cold spell   a period of very cold weather
also: **cold snap**
opposite meaning: **heat wave** (a period of very hot weather)

- The city government had to open shelters for homeless people during the long *cold spell.*
- Farmers have to worry about frost damage to their crops during severe *cold snaps.*
- During a *heat wave*, people either use air-conditioning or open all their windows.

roll in   to approach from a distance, over land or sea
    opposite meaning: **roll (back) out (to sea)**
    USAGE NOTE: *Roll (back) out (to sea)* is used when coastal fog recedes from the land.
    ■ The thunderstorm **rolled in** suddenly and dropped two inches of rain.
    ■ The planes were not allowed to take off from the airport after the fog **rolled in.**
    ■ Most flights were delayed several hours until the fog **rolled back out to sea.**

die down   to reduce in strength, to diminish, to subside
    also: **let up**
    USAGE NOTE: These idioms can also be used to refer to sounds.
    ■ We were lucky that the blizzard **died down** enough so that we could ski.
    ■ After several hours of heavy downpour, the rain finally **let up.**
    ■ The thunder **died down** as the storm moved out of the area.

clear up   to become sunny
    ■ It was cloudy all morning, but in the afternoon it **cleared up** completely.
    ■ The weather **cleared up** nicely when the fog rolled out to sea.

dry up   to become dry, to lose moisture
    also: **dry out**
    USAGE NOTE: *Dry out* applies to things that are not normally used when they are wet.
    ■ Streams and small lakes can **dry up** during periods of drought.
    ■ It took a long time for the soccer field to **dry out** after the heavy rains.

EXERCISES

A.   **Fill in each blank with the part of the idiom that is missing.**

Cold Arctic storms can greatly affect the weather when they roll _____
₁ along the coastline of Northern California. Sometimes it _____ cats and dogs
₂ for days before the weather finally clears _____. When this happens, water
₃ that runs _____ the hills and mountains can cause serious flooding.
₄

Arctic storms are sometimes associated with _____ spells during which
₅ temperatures _____ down considerably, and crops may suffer damage. Some
₆ of the storms may reach Southern California, but generally they have died
_____ by that point.
₇

After the winter storm season, the temperature begins to heat _____
₈ again, and the ground starts to dry out. During unusually warm periods, small
lakes and streams _____ up quickly.
₉

B. **Choose the statement in the right column that best responds to each question in the left column. Write the appropriate number in the blank.**

NOTE: *To do this as a listening exercise, cover up the left column before you start the tape.*

1. Has it cooled off yet outside?	____ a. Maybe we could build a wall in back to control the water.
2. What's that loud noise on the roof?	____ b. No, this heat wave is keeping temperatures high all day.
3. How can we stop the runoff from the hill behind our house?	____ c. I think it's the sound of rain beating down.
4. Do you want to play ball on the lawn?	____ d. It sure did. It never seemed to let up.
5. Didn't it rain cats and dogs last night?	____ e. We shouldn't until the grass dries out.

C. **Use the idioms in your spoken or written answers to the following questions.**

1. How could you tell that a storm was going to *roll in?*
2. Have you ever been outside in a storm where it *rained cats and dogs?* What did you do to protect yourself?
3. During a *cold snap* in your country, how low can the temperature get?
4. During a *heat wave* in your country, how high can the temperature get?
5. What happens outside when the weather begins to *clear up?*

D. **Using the idioms from this unit, develop a presentation describing the weather in your native country. You may include the following information:**

- in which month the weather begins to heat up for summer;
- in which month the weather begins to cool off for winter;
- whether your country is more likely to have heat waves or cold spells, and when they occur;
- how often storms roll in and how quickly the weather clears up.

Review: Units 1–10

A. Circle the expression that best completes each sentence.

1. The Masons really _____ on their big night on the town.
   a. had a ball
   b. gave someone a lift
   c. hit the sack

2. The angry visitors were not able to _____ the hotel because it was booked up.
   a. check out of
   b. soak in
   c. check into

3. The closets are filled with things we don't need. We should have a _____ soon.
   a. garage sale
   b. rush hour
   c. housekeeper

4. Oscar was so tired out that he _____ on the couch.
   a. stayed up
   b. fell asleep
   c. put away

5. Max doesn't clock in until eleven o'clock at night because he works the _____.
   a. graveyard shift
   b. blue-collar
   c. odds and ends

6. I don't want to get up yet. Let's _____ until noon.
   a. put back
   b. sleep in
   c. loosen up

7. Mrs. Evans will _____ from her business trip early next week.
   a. get off
   b. get ready
   c. get back

8. The drive didn't take as long as I expected because we _____.
   a. had free time
   b. took a breather
   c. made good time

9. Corinne drank a big cup of coffee to _____ this morning.
   a. get herself going
   b. go off
   c. give someone a ride

10. I think that Mr. Coleman _____ as a professional ice-hockey player.
    a. does a living
    b. earns a living
    c. calls it a day

B. Indicate whether each statement is TRUE (T) or FALSE (F).

_____ 1. You might turn in late if you're throwing a party.

_____ 2. When a storm lets up, the wind probably dies down.

_____ 3. To ride shotgun, you get in the driver's seat.

_____ 4. Some people get themselves going in the morning by taking a shower.

_____ 5. A night owl would want to wake up at the crack of dawn.

_____ 6. The ground starts to dry out when the runoff has stopped.

_____ 7. If someone in your family is going away, it might be nice to see them off.

_____ 8. The carpool lane is a good place to double-park during rush hour.

_____ 9. Doing the dishes is one way of cleaning out the kitchen.

_____ 10. You wouldn't mind dropping someone off at a place that was on your way.

C. Complete the puzzle with the missing parts of the idioms in the sentences below.

ACROSS

4. Do you get out and _____ much now?
6. A plumber is a blue-_____ worker.
8. Why did you _____ out so late last night?
9. Only a party _____ would stay up so late.
10. Do the _____ before you watch TV.

DOWN

1. Always _____ up when you drive.
2. A gas-_____ wastes a lot of fuel.
3. We've been working too hard. It's time to take a _____.
5. How do you get _____ without a car?
6. The air is fresh at the _____ of dawn.
7. Does it _____ cats and dogs very often?
8. I didn't _____ a wink because of my cold.

31

Unit 11
Small Talk

shake hands   to greet someone by taking that person's hand and shaking it
also: **shake someone's hand**

- When you meet someone for the first time, it's polite to *shake hands.*
- Your close friends are unlikely to *shake your hand* when you meet.

not see for ages   not to meet someone for a long time
also: **not see in ages**

Grammar Note: Use the present perfect tense or past perfect tense.

- Do you know where John has been? I *haven't seen* him *for ages.*
- Karin returned home for Christmas because she *hadn't seen* her parents *in ages.*

a sight for sore eyes   someone or something you're glad to see again

- Fabio, you're *a sight for sore eyes!* I missed you while you were gone.
- After Denise returned from a long business trip, her own bed was *a sight for sore eyes.*

Long time no see   an expression to show that a long time has passed since you saw someone last

- Is that you, Alice? I can't believe it. *Long time no see!*

strike up a conversation   to begin talking with someone for the first time

- A crowded elevator is an awkward place to *strike up a conversation.*
- As Linda waited at the bus stop, she *struck up a conversation* with a woman standing next to her.

make small talk   to talk about common topics such as the weather, activities, family, and work
also: **make conversation**

- Shinji isn't good at *making small talk* at parties. He's usually quiet and just listens.
- The professor *made conversation* with her students before class started.

break the ice   to end an awkward situation by suggesting a topic of conversation
related form: *icebreaker* (noun)

- When the hostess introduced Igor at the party, there was a moment of silence until she *broke the ice* by saying, "Did you know that Igor is an Olympic silver medalist?"
- Jobs or hobbies are good *icebreakers* when you can't think of anything to talk about.

shoot the breeze   to talk or chat casually
also: **chew the fat**

- ▪ Tom met his friends at the golf club for lunch and to *shoot the breeze.*
- ▪ Some office workers avoid getting their work done by *chewing the fat* with co-workers.

What's going on?   What's happening?
also: **What's new?, What's up?**

USAGE NOTE: A common response is *Not much* or *Nothing special.*

- ▪ PERSON 1: Hi, Michelle. *What's going on?*

  PERSON 2: Not much, Jorge.

- ▪ PERSON 1: *What's new*, Karla?

  PERSON 2: Nothing special, Pete. *What's up* with you?

So long   good-bye, farewell
also: **Take it easy, Take care**

- ▪ TANYA: I've got to go, Jack. *So long.*

  JACK: *So long*, Tanya.

- ▪ SARAH: Well, Junko, time to go. *Take it easy.*

  JUNKO: *Take care*, Sarah.

Catch you later   good-bye, with the idea of seeing someone at a later time
also: **See you around**

GRAMMAR NOTE: The subject pronoun *I* + *will* can be used with these idioms. If it is not used, it is implied.

- ▪ Oh no, I'm late for my appointment. *Catch you later.*
- ▪ I'm glad you've enrolled in school again. I'll *see you around!*

EXERCISES

A.   **Fill in each blank with the missing part of the idiom.**

1. Marcia, is that really you? What a _____ for sore eyes!

2. Topics such as family, work, and hobbies are good ways to break the _____ when you meet someone for the first time.

3. I can't believe it's you, Simone. _____ time no see!

4. Tina greeted Mike by asking, "What's _____ on?"

5. Sam is happy to be with his sister again. He hasn't _____ her for ages.

6. I'm already late for class. _____ long!

7. Kim is good at making _____ talk. She usually has something interesting to say.

8. During a break, workers like to stand around and _____ the breeze.

9. As Alan ran out the front door, he yelled back, "_____ you later!"

10. José tried to _____ up a conversation with a girl he really wanted to meet.

11. After the businessmen signed the agreement, they shook _____.

B. Choose the statement in the right column that best responds to each question in the left column. Write the appropriate number in the blank.

 NOTE: *To do this as a listening exercise, cover up the left column before you start the tape.*

1. Nancy, is that really you?
2. Can't you stay and chew the fat a while longer?
3. Hey, Larry. What's up?
4. Do you want to go to the party tonight?
5. Did you strike up a conversation with that actress you wanted to meet?

____ a. No, I really have to go. See you around.

____ b. Not really. I'm not very good at making conversation.

____ c. Yes, and I even shook her hand and got her autograph.

____ d. Yes, it is, Joe. Long time no see!

____ e. Nothing special.

C. Use the idioms in your spoken or written answers to the following questions.

1. Is it easy for you to *strike up a conversation* with a stranger? Why or why not?
2. How good are you at *making small talk*, even with people you know well?
3. Jobs and hobbies are good *icebreakers* when you first meet someone. What are some other possible topics to *break the ice?*
4. What are some differences in the way that people around the world, both young and old, *shake hands?*
5. Is there anyone that you *haven't seen for ages?* Who? Would that person be *a sight for sore eyes?*

D. Using the idioms from this unit, develop a dialogue or role play about meeting someone you haven't seen for a long time. You may include the following information:

- how long it has been since you've seen the person;
- whether you shake hands;
- whether he or she is a sight for sore eyes;
- what you say to shoot the breeze;
- how you say good-bye.

Unit 12
On the Telephone

make a (phone) call   to use the telephone

 USAGE NOTE: Adjectives such as *important* and *quick* are often added to this idiom.

 ■ The manager went to her office to **make an** important **phone call.**

 ■ Jonah had to **make a** quick **call** before he left home.

be on the phone   to be using the telephone
 opposite meaning: **be off the phone**

 ■ Ms. Quintana **is on the phone** right now. She'll be available in a moment.

 ■ As soon as I**'m off the phone**, I'll check the information for you.

over the phone   by using the telephone
 also: **on the phone**

 USAGE NOTE: These expressions are used to show exactly how contact between two people is made. They are used with verbs such as *give, talk,* and *speak,* but not *be.*

 ■ Instead of sending a fax, the assistant gave her boss the information
   over the phone.

 ■ The doctor and his patient spoke **on the phone** about the medical problem.

call up   to telephone someone
 also: **give someone a call**

 GRAMMAR NOTE: *Call up* is separable.

 ■ You should **call up** Carmen before she **calls** Carlos **up.**

 ■ Why haven't you **given** her **a call** yet?

hold on   to wait for assistance on the telephone
 related form: **on hold**

 ■ The telephone operator asked the caller to **hold on** while she transferred the call.

 ■ I was **on hold** for several minutes because the clerks were busy with customers.

off the hook   not placed properly on the base unit of the telephone
 opposite meaning: **on the hook**

 USAGE NOTE: This idiom means that the telephone handset is not properly placed on the base unit. The opposite form *on the hook* is less often used.

 ■ Carl left the telephone **off the hook** so that he wouldn't be bothered by any calls.

 ■ Please put the phone back **on the hook** so that we can be reached.

call back   to telephone someone who has just called and left a message, to call again
also: **return someone's call**

GRAMMAR NOTE: *Call back* is separable, so the object may follow the verb.

- Craig **called back** Alice as soon as he got her message.
- However, when he **called** her **back**, she wasn't at home.
- He left a message for her to **return his call.**
- I asked Frank to **call** me **back** because I was too busy to talk.

hang up   to put the telephone handset back on the base unit at the end of a call

USAGE NOTE: This idiom may be used with or without an object. The idiom is separable if an object is used.

- The salesperson shouldn't have **hung** the phone **up** before I could ask another question.
- Todd was enjoying his talk with an old friend so much that he didn't want to **hang up.**

crank call   a telephone call intended only to annoy or bother someone

- Sometimes small children use the telephone to make **crank calls.**
- Kyle hung up the phone right away when she realized that it was a **crank call.**

EXERCISES

A. **Fill in each blank with the missing part of the idiom.**

AMY: Why is the phone off the _____, Dan?
                                          1

DAN: Oh, I got a _____ call a while ago.
                          2

AMY: What did you do—just _____ up on the person?
                                          3

DAN: Yes, but he _____ back almost immediately.
                          4

AMY: What did he want?

DAN: I guess just to annoy someone over the _____.
                                                          5

AMY: Strange! Anyway, I need to _____ a call.
                                          6

DAN: Sure, Amy. How long will you be _____ the phone?
                                                      7

AMY: I just need to call _____ the airline to make a reservation.
                                  8

DAN: In that case, you'll probably get a recorded message and have to

          _____on for several minutes until an agent is available.
                  9

B. Choose the statement in the right column that best responds to each question in the left column. Write the appropriate number in the blank.

NOTE: *To do this as a listening exercise, cover up the left column before you start the tape.*

1. Would you like me to give you a call next week?

2. Is Myrna still on the phone?

3. Could you tell Sandra that I gave her a call?

4. Has your phone been off the hook?

5. Would you mind holding on while I check the chicken in the oven?

____ a. I surely will, and I'll ask her to return your call soon.

____ b. Yes. Call me up next Monday.

____ c. Yes, I forgot to put it back on the hook after the last call.

____ d. Of course not. But if you take too long, I'll hang up!

____ e. No, she's been off the phone for a few minutes.

C. Use the idioms in your spoken or written answers to the following questions.

1. Have you ever *hung up* on someone before? Why might you do this?
2. Give some examples of information you could get *over the phone.*
3. Have you ever received a *crank call?* What did you do?
4. What do you do if you have to *make a phone call* when you're not at home?
5. When would an office receptionist put a caller *on hold?*

D. Using the idioms from this unit, develop a dialogue or role play about a day when you make a lot of phone calls. You may include the following information:

- how many phone calls you make;
- the people or businesses you call up;
- whether anyone puts you on hold;
- whether someone says he or she will call you back;
- how long you are on the phone.

Unit 13
Communicating

drop someone a line   to mail a letter to someone
- Larry *dropped* Angela *a line* so that she would know where he moved.
- Why don't you *drop* me *a line* some time to let me know how you're doing?

dash off   to write a quick letter or note to someone
also: **get off**

GRAMMAR/USAGE NOTES: These idioms are separable, and are used when something is written in a hurry or at the last possible moment.
- Mrs. Sato *dashed off* a note to her husband before heading to work.
- Sam *got off* a birthday card to his brother with no time to spare.

hear from   to receive a letter or phone call from someone
- Have you *heard from* Marco since he left on his trip?
- It's so good to *hear from* you again, Bernice!

be in touch (with)   to have contact or communication with someone
opposite meaning: **be out of touch (with)**

USAGE NOTE: Both idioms can also be used with the verbs *keep* and *stay*.
- Don't worry. I'll *be in touch with* you early tomorrow morning.
- My high school friends and I have *kept in touch* over the years through correspondence.
- Just because you're moving, it doesn't mean that we can't *stay in touch.*
- While camping alone in the mountains, Yoshio *was out of touch* with everyone.

get in touch with   to contact, to reach
also: **get ahold of, touch base with**

GRAMMAR NOTE: The word *base* can be either singular or plural.
- My office assistant can *get in touch with* me in an emergency.
- Do you know how to *get ahold of* Fred? I've lost his number.
- The Madisons asked their daughter to *touch base with* them often while away at school.

get back to   to contact someone again

     also: **get back with**

- As soon as I receive more information about the party, I'll **get back to** you.
- The manager said that she'd **get back with** the salesperson as soon as she had decided what furniture to buy.

talk a mile a minute   to talk very quickly

     also: **speak a mile a minute**

- Some TV and radio commercials are difficult to understand because the people are **talking a mile a minute.**
- When you visit a foreign country and don't know the language, everyone seems to be **speaking a mile a minute.**

bend someone's ear   to talk for a long time without much interruption

     also: **talk someone's ear off**

     USAGE NOTE: These idioms are used when someone is being forced to listen.

- Ali kept saying that it was late, but the visitor **bent his ear** for over two hours.
- How could Mark **talk my ear off** like that when he knew I was sick?

yackety-yak   meaningless noise or uninteresting conversation

- All I heard was a lot of **yackety-yak** when I entered the crowded room.
- When someone bends your ear, you can say that it's just a bunch of **yackety-yak.**

junk mail   generally unwanted information sent through the mail by businesses

- Some people don't mind looking at **junk mail**, while others hate to receive it.
- You can be sure that the postal delivery persons don't like to carry **junk mail!**

EXERCISES

A.   **Fill in each blank with the missing part of the idiom.**

1. When I finally make my decision, I'll get _____ to you right away.

2. Kayoko has been able to keep in _____ with most of her high school friends.

3. Fred was happy when he _____ from his old friend Larry after so many years.

4. Two days before her birthday, Martin dashed _____ a quick note to his sister.

5. Khalid and Sonya left the party early because they were tired of listening to all the _____-yak.

6. Mr. Murillo hates to see _____ mail when he checks his mailbox.

7. Make sure you don't sit next to Ernie or he'll bend your _____ all night.

8. Another problem with Ernie is that he talks a _____ a minute.

9. Did you _____ in touch with the Highway Department and complain about the large holes in the road by our house?

10. I can't remember the last time that I dropped Tiffany a _____. I'd better write to her soon.

B. Choose the statement in the right column that best responds to each question in the left column. Write the appropriate number in the blank.

NOTE: *To do this as a listening exercise, cover up the left column before you start the tape.*

1. Doesn't it seem that everyone at this party is talking a mile a minute?

2. How can I get ahold of Mrs. Atkinson?

3. Haven't you heard about the big earthquake in Chile?

4. Would you like me to drop you a line after I get home?

5. Do you know the date for the meeting?

____ a. I have her number right here in my directory.

____ b. You're right. There sure is a lot of yackety-yak going on.

____ c. No, we were out of touch with everything while camping.

____ d. I'm not sure. I'll get back with you later about it.

____ e. Sure. It's important to stay in touch.

C. Use the idioms in your spoken or written answers to the following questions.

1. Who's the last person that you've *heard from?*

2. Who's the last person that you *dashed off* a note to? Did he or she *get* a reply *off* to you?

3. Have you *been out of touch with* anyone for a long time? Who?

4. What can you do when someone is *talking your ear off?*

5. Do you mind receiving *junk mail?* Why or why not?

D. Using the idioms from this unit, tell a classmate about communicating with relatives. You may include the following information:

- who you are often in touch with, and who you are usually out of touch with;
- which relative you enjoy hearing from the most;
- whether you take time to write letters or dash them off instead;
- who in your family speaks a mile a minute, or makes a lot of yackety-yak.

Unit 14
School

sign up (for)   to register (for), to enroll (in)

GRAMMAR/USAGE NOTES: People who cannot sign up for themselves become the object of the verb. In this case the idiom is separable. The idiom is often used for sports activities.

- The Smith's seventeen-year-old son *signed up for* classes at the public university.
- Laura *signed* her son *up for* a gymnastics class at the recreation center.
- If you want to get on the volleyball team, it's not too late to *sign up.*

hit the books   to study, sometimes after much delay

- Students have no choice but to *hit the books* before taking their final exams.

brush up on   to review

also: **bone up on**

USAGE NOTE: *Bone up on* is more informal than *brush up on.*

- As you learn new vocabulary, it's good to *brush up on* it regularly.
- The medical student had to *bone up on* the respiratory system before her oral exams.

pop quiz   a short, unannounced test

- There may be a couple of *pop quizzes* this semester in addition to the regular exams.
- All the students became worried when the teacher announced a *pop quiz.*

hand in   to submit

also: **turn in**

GRAMMAR NOTE: Both idioms are separable.

- Please *hand in* your homework before you leave the classroom.
- The professor *turned* his course grades *in* to the admissions and records office.

hand out   to distribute

also: **pass out**

related form: **handout** (noun)

GRAMMAR NOTE: The two verb forms are separable.

- On the first day of classes, the professor *handed out* the course syllabus.
- Politicians and salespersons are allowed on campus to *pass* flyers *out*.
- I've been given so many *handouts* this semester that there's no room in my notebook!

teacher's pet   someone who seems to be the teacher's favorite student

- I think that Jonathan got an *A* because he's the *teacher's pet.*
- The *teacher's pet* is usually a student who gets special treatment and privileges.

cut class(es)   to not attend class(es)

also: **play hooky, ditch school**

GRAMMAR/USAGE NOTES: *Class* can be either singular or plural. The alternate forms are used when missing school is against the rules.

- Aaron and Yousef *cut classes* on Friday in order to have a three-day weekend.
- The troublesome teenagers *played hooky* for two days, but when they tried to *ditch school* for a third day, they were caught and punished.

drop out (of)   to stop attending regularly

also: **flunk out (of)**

related form: **dropout** (noun)

USAGE NOTE: *Flunk out* is used when the reason for dropping out is failing grades.

- Michael had to *drop out of* school in order to work full-time.
- When Judy *flunked out of* high school with bad grades, she became another *dropout.*

EXERCISES

A.   **Fill in each blank with the missing part of the idiom.**

1. None of the students got an *A* on the _____ quiz we had yesterday.

2. The teacher handed _____ a special notice about a school activity.

3. Before traveling to Mexico, Deena brushed _____ on her Spanish.

4. The easiest place for me to hit the _____ is in the library.

5. Louis _____ up for the tennis team when he enrolled in college.

6. Teenagers who _____ out of high school after two or three years generally work at lower-paying jobs than teenagers who succeed in graduating.

7. The police questioned the group of kids in the park who were cutting _____.

8. When the test period ended, the students handed _____ their work.

9. If you keep writing notes to your teacher like that, you'll soon become the teacher's _____.

B. Choose the statement in the right column that best responds to each question in the left column. Write the appropriate number in the blank.

NOTE: *To do this as a listening exercise, cover up the left column before you start the tape.*

1. Did you hear that Tom dropped out of school?

2. What do you think about ditching school today and going to the beach?

3. When should I turn in my research project?

4. When do you want to get together and hit the books?

5. Why does the teacher ask Amanda to help her so much?

____ a. You should hand it in by the end of the month.

____ b. Yes, but actually I believe that he flunked out!

____ c. I can't cut classes. I have an important test this afternoon.

____ d. Don't you know? She's the new teacher's pet.

____ e. Let's bone up on the material tomorrow night, OK?

C. Use the idioms in your spoken or written answers to the following questions.

1. What kinds of materials does a teacher **hand out?**
2. During what part of the day do you prefer to **hit the books?** Why?
3. Give some reasons why a student might have to **drop out of** school.
4. Should teachers give **pop quizzes?** Why or why not?
5. What kinds of activities do people **sign up for?**

D. Using the idioms from this unit, develop a dialogue or role play about a day at school. You may include the following information:

- what classes you are signed up for;
- whether there is a lot of homework to turn in;
- how often you have to hit the books;
- whether anyone in your class is the teacher's pet;
- where you keep the teacher's handouts.

Unit 15
Shopping

pick up to buy, to purchase

GRAMMAR/USAGE NOTES: This idiom is separable. It is often used for shopping briefly at a grocery store or supermarket.

- Could you go to the store quickly and *pick up* some milk? We don't have any more.
- I *picked* a few things *up* at the supermarket on my way home from work.

pick out to select, to choose

GRAMMAR NOTE: The idiom is separable.

- I tried to *pick out* the larger, riper apples in the produce section.
- Sheila asked her mom to go with her to *pick* some new clothes *out*.

on sale at a reduced cost

- By buying things when they're *on sale*, it's possible to save a lot of money.
- I asked the clerk, "Do these expensive watches ever go *on sale?*"

hunt for bargains to look for the cheapest prices
related form: **bargain-hunter** (noun)

- The week after Christmas is the best time to *hunt for bargains*.
- *Bargain-hunters* like to shop in thrift stores such as the Family Discount Chain.

shop around to check further on cost, quality, and so on before buying
also: **look around**

- I *shopped around* at several stores before finding the refrigerator I wanted.
- My wife asked me, "Shouldn't we *look around* more before deciding what to get?"

window-shop to look at merchandise in stores without buying anything
also: **go window-shopping**

- It's fun to get together with a friend and *window-shop*.
- When Carol doesn't have extra money, she loves to go *window-shopping*.

buy up to buy all available items
also: **snap up**

- Just before the hurricane, people *bought up* all the bottled water in the stores.
- On the day of the big sale, all the best items were *snapped up* first.

raincheck a receipt to purchase an unavailable sale item later at the sale price

USAGE NOTE: When a business sells all of a particular sale item, it offers rainchecks to customers so that they can buy the item when it becomes available later, still at the sale price.

- Umberto asked the cashier for a **raincheck** because the sale item he wanted was all gone.
- Could I please have a **raincheck** for a ten-pound bag of dog food at half price?

stock up (on) to purchase extra amounts for later use
also: **load up (on)**

- Department stores always **stock up on** gift items before Christmas.
- After experiencing a serious oil shortage years ago, oil companies are careful to **stock up.**
- People who live in very cold places **load up on** firewood before winter arrives.

take back to return merchandise to a store
also: **bring back**

GRAMMAR/USAGE NOTES: Both idioms are separable. *Take back* is generally used when talking outside the store, *bring back* when talking inside the store.

- Louie couldn't **take back** the jacket he bought because it was on sale.
- Can I **bring** this compact disc player **back** if I'm not satisfied with it?

EXERCISES

A. **Fill in each blank with the missing part of the idiom.**

INEZ: Would you like to go _____-shopping at the mall today?
                                                   ₁

RUTH: You know we never just window-shop. One of us always _____
            ₂

something up that's on _____.
           ₃

INEZ: I know. But at least we always _____ for bargains.
            ₄

RUTH: Like the time we bought _____ all those cheap woolen socks!
            ₅

INEZ: Don't remind me of that! We thought it would be a good idea to

_____ up on warm clothing before winter.
       ₆

RUTH: Until we discovered how poorly the socks were made. Didn't we

_____ most of them back to the store?
       ₇

INEZ: We sure did. Oh, look at this ad. Haven't you been shopping _____
                 ₈

for a new shower curtain?

RUTH: Yes, but I haven't found a nice one so far. These look good—and what

a reasonable price!

INEZ: So let's go and _____ out a nice one together.
            ₉

RUTH: At this price, they've probably all gone.

INEZ: If that's true, we'll just ask for a _____.
                   ₁₀

B. Choose the statement in the right column that best responds to each question in the left column. Write the appropriate number in the blank.

NOTE: *To do this as a listening exercise, cover up the left column before you start the tape.*

1. Would you like to window-shop at the center this afternoon?

____ a. Perfect. Window-shopping is the only thing I can afford to do.

2. Were you able to find the bedsheets that were on sale?

____ b. I looked around but I didn't see anything I liked.

3. Why did you load up on so many canned goods and bottles of water?

____ c. Unfortunately, they'd all been bought up.

4. Are these shoes good enough to use for jogging?

____ d. I don't think so. Try to pick out some better ones.

5. Did you pick anything up at the clothing store?

____ e. I thought we should stock up in case there's an emergency.

C. Use the idioms in your spoken or written answers to the following questions.

1. What was the last thing you *picked up* at the store?
2. In the United States, it is very easy to *take* something *back* to a store. Is this true in your country? Why or why not?
3. Is there any system of giving *rainchecks* in your country? What do you think of this system?
4. Are you a *bargain-hunter?* Why or why not?
5. What items should you *stock up on* to prepare for a serious emergency?

D. Using the idioms from this unit, tell a classmate about your last shopping trip. You may include the following information:

- what items you picked up;
- whether anyone helped you pick out the items;
- what items were on sale;
- whether any items you wanted had already been snapped up;
- whether you had to take any of the items back to the store later.

Unit 16
Eating and Dining

eat out   to eat a meal prepared at a restaurant
  also: **grab a bite to eat**
  opposite meaning: **eat in** (to eat at home)
  USAGE NOTE: *Grab a bite to eat* is used to talk about a quick meal or snack.
  - Every Saturday night the Thompsons *eat out* at their favorite restaurant.
  - Let's *grab a bite to eat* on the way to the theater, OK?
  - It's been a long day. Why don't we *eat in* tonight?

take out   to leave a restaurant with the food instead of eating it there
  also: **carry out, to go**
  GRAMMAR NOTE: *Take out* and *carry out* are separable.
  - Many restaurants allow you to *take out* the food on their menus.
  - Umberto decided to *carry* his dinner *out* rather than eat in the restaurant.
  - Sir, is this order for here or *to go?*

junk food   food that has poor nutritional value
  - Fast-food restaurants are the most familiar places that serve *junk food.*
  - Hamburgers, french fries, and milkshakes are typical examples of *junk food.*

eat up   to eat completely, to devour
  also: **gobble up**
  GRAMMAR/USAGE NOTES: Both forms are separable. *Gobble up* generally refers to the act of eating very quickly.
  - The boys were so hungry that they *ate up* all the hot dogs in a couple of minutes.
  - John *gobbled* the food *up* without even saying a word.

leftovers   food that remains uneaten from a meal
  related form: **be left over** (verb)
  - I usually cook extra food for dinner and then save the *leftovers* for snacks and other meals.
  - Judy expected some food to *be left over* from Thanksgiving, but it was all eaten.

doggy bag   a special container for taking uneaten food from a restaurant
  - If some food is left over from a restaurant meal, you can ask for a *doggy bag* to take it with you.
  - A *doggy bag* can be anything from a nice plastic container to a simple foil wrapper.

Unit 16

pot luck   a meal where each invited person contributes one item of food

GRAMMAR NOTE: This idiom can be hyphenated to form an adjective. (In some dictionaries, this idiom is spelled as one word.)

- Sarah enjoys going to *pot lucks* because there is always such a variety of food.
- A *pot-luck* picnic is a popular activity in the summertime.

pig out   to eat too much food
also: **stuff one's face**

Usage Note: Both idioms are used informally.

- After I've *pigged out* on ice cream at night, I always regret it the next day.
- It's impolite to *stuff your face* in front of other people, especially guests.

wolf down   to eat or drink very quickly
also: **gulp down**

GRAMMAR/USAGE NOTES: Both idioms are separable. *Wolf down* is used for food and drink in general. *Gulp down* is generally used for drink.

- Ulrike *wolfed down* her breakfast before leaving for work.
- *Gulping down* cold water while you're exercising can cause a stomachache.

have a sweet tooth   to enjoy eating sweet foods such as candies and desserts

USAGE NOTE: Adverbs such as *quite* and adjectives such as *bad* can be added.

- Joan always has a supply of chocolates on her desk. She *has* quite *a sweet tooth*.
- Ted is overweight because he *has a* bad *sweet tooth*.

EXERCISES

A.   **Fill in each blank with the missing part of the idiom.**

1. For lunch today Tami had some spaghetti _____ from dinner two days ago.

2. Why don't we rent a movie and take _____ some Chinese food?

3. I don't feel like cooking tonight. Let's _____ out at Benny's instead.

4. People who are serious about their diets don't eat much _____ food.

5. Waiter, could I please have a _____ bag for this steak I couldn't finish?

6. Pedro was so hungry after exercising that he wolfed _____ a whole pizza.

7. An all-you-can-eat buffet is a good place to go if you like to _____ out.

8. Helen made a large tossed salad for the pot _____ at her church.

9. I can't believe that the two of us ate _____ all of that large pizza.

10. Robert will love these cookies. He has quite a _____ tooth.

B. Choose the statement in the right column that best responds to each question in the left column. Write the appropriate number in the blank.

NOTE: *To do this as a listening exercise, cover up the left column before you start the tape.*

1. Why does Betty always have chocolate in her desk?

2. What are you going to take to the pot luck?

3. All the potato chips are gone! Did you stuff your face again?

4. Would you like to grab a bite to eat somewhere?

5. Should I ask for a doggy bag for these leftover french fries?

____ a. I thought I'd make a chicken casserole.

____ b. Why bother? It's not worth saving junk food.

____ c. I'd prefer to carry something out, if that's OK with you.

____ d. I'm sorry. I gobbled them up before I realized it.

____ e. She has a terrible sweet tooth.

C. Use the idioms in your spoken or written answers to the following questions.

1. Do you **have a sweet tooth?** What kinds of sweet things do you like?

2. What kind of **junk food** do you like, if any? Do you worry about its nutritional value? Why or why not?

3. Is it healthy to **wolf down** food? Why or why not?

4. Explain the advantages and disadvantages of **taking out** rather than **eating out**.

5. What kinds of food do people bring to a **pot luck?** Have you ever been to one?

D. Using the idioms from this unit, tell a classmate about your eating habits. You may include the following information:

- how often you eat out each week;
- how often you get food to take out;
- whether you generally eat up your food or if there are leftovers;
- when (if ever) you have to wolf down your food;
- when (if ever) you pig out.

Unit 17
Family

come from   to originate from a place
also: **be from**

GRAMMAR/USAGE NOTES: These idioms refer to one's present or past homeland. When referring to one's present homeland, only the simple present tense is used.

- ■ Most of the students in my class **come from** Asia.
- ■ Patrick's ancestors all **came from** Scotland 200 years ago.
- ■ I'**m from** Uruguay. Where **are** you **from?**

grow up   1) to develop from a child into an adult 2) to mature
related form: **grown-up** (noun form meaning "adult")

USAGE NOTE: *Grow up* has two meanings. The first refers to natural physical development from child to adult. The second refers to reasonable, mature behavior.

- ■ Mike was born in New York, but **grew up** in California.
- ■ My fourteen-year-old son still acts foolishly. I hope he **grows up** soon.
- ■ Small children need the constant supervision of **grown-ups.**

bring up   to raise, to rear, to educate

GRAMMAR/USAGE NOTES: This idiom is separable. Note how it differs from *grow up* above: Children *grow up* (no object); parents *bring up* children (object).

- ■ Martina is a well-adjusted child. Her parents have **brought** her **up** carefully.
- ■ It's sometimes difficult to **bring up** children in today's society.

flesh and blood   one's relatives and immediate family

USAGE NOTE: This idiom often is preceded by *one's own* . . . .

- ■ All of our **flesh and blood** came to the big family reunion.
- ■ Sue doesn't want to tell the police about her brother's crime because he's her own *flesh and blood.*

take after   to resemble, to look like (for physical appearance)
also: **be a chip off the old block**

USAGE NOTE: *Take after* can refer to similarities in personality or physical appearance. *Be a chip off the old block* is used when two people in a family share the same characteristics in personality.

- ■ Did you notice how Kate **takes after** her father in personality, but her mother in looks?
- ■ Larry is about as lazy as his father. He's just a *chip off the old block.*

settle down   to begin a regular, stable life
also: **put down roots**
USAGE NOTE: These idioms are used when someone who often moves or travels a lot finally decides to live a more normal life in one place. *Settle down* is also used for people who have lived active social lives but are ready to limit their activities.

- Teresa's family moved from state to state until finally they *settled down* in Arizona.
- After years of travelling and partying, Jason decided to *settle down* and have a family.
- My ancestors *put down roots* in America over a century ago.

hand down   to give from one generation to the next
also: **pass down**
related form: **hand-me-down** (noun)
GRAMMAR NOTE: The pronoun *me* in *hand-me-down* cannot change form in any way.

- I still have the old stamp collection that my grandfather *handed down* to me.
- In every society, important traditions are *passed down* from generation to generation.
- Nancy has kept every *hand-me-down* that her relatives have ever given her.

give birth (to)   to bear a child
also: **have a child, have a (baby) boy/girl**

- Mrs. Larsen's family was surprised when she *gave birth to* twins.
- Have you and your husband decided whether you're ready to *have a child* yet?
- My sister just *had a baby boy*. I'm an uncle!

EXERCISES

A.   Fill in each blank with the missing part of the idiom.

1. John is having too much fun as a single person. He's not ready to get married and _____ down.

2. Isn't it amazing how Giselle _____ after her grandfather instead of her father?

3. Steve showed us some old family photographs that were handed _____ to him.

4. The criminal was so bad that he even stole from his own _____ and blood.

5. Alexandra has such a nice personality for an eight-year-old. Her parents have really _____ her up well.

6. Most of the students in my English-language classes come _____ Asia.

7. Valerie _____ up on the West Coast before her family moved to New York.

8. Mrs. Lindstrom gave _____ to a ten-pound baby.

B. Choose the statement in the right column that best responds to each question in the left column. Write the appropriate number in the blank.

NOTE: *To do this as a listening exercise, cover up the left column before you start the tape.*

1. Is Linda going to have a child or is she just getting fat?
2. Can I go to the party at Narong's house this weekend?
3. Are you ready to put down roots in this community?
4. Are you from Japan?
5. Isn't Amy good at drawing, like her father?

____ a. Yes, I've finally decided to settle down here.

____ b. Yes, she's a chip off the old block.

____ c. No, I come from Taiwan.

____ d. Yes, if there's going to be at least one grown-up there.

____ e. She's heavy because she's going to give birth in September.

C. Use the idioms in your spoken or written answers to the following questions.

1. Who do you consider your *flesh and blood?*
2. Who do you take after more—your mother or your father? If you have brothers and sisters, who do they *take after?*
3. What *hand-me-downs* do you have, and who *passed* them *down* to you?
4. If you could choose any place in the world, where would you most like to *settle down?* Why?
5. Are you interested in getting married and *having a child?* Why or why not?

D. Using the idioms from this unit, develop a presentation about your family background. You may include the following information:

- which country you come from;
- whether you also grew up in this country;
- which country your parents came from, if different from your own;
- which of your flesh and blood was most responsible for bringing you up;
- who you take after in personality;
- who you take after in appearance.

Unit 18
Dating and Friendship

go out (with)   to date, to accompany socially on a single date
also: **take someone out**

GRAMMAR NOTE: *Take out* is separable.

- Dave wanted to *go out with* the new girl at school, but he was too shy to ask.
- Mr. Nguyen *took* his fiancée *out* to a fancy restaurant on her birthday.

go with   to date on a regular basis
also: **go steady (with)**

USAGE NOTE: *Go steady* is not commonly used by younger people. *Go out with* can also be used for a series of dates.

- Ulla has been *going with* Sven for several months.
- Frank lets his girlfriend wear his jacket because they're *going steady.*
- How long have you been *going out with* your friendly neighbor?

blind date   a date with a person whom one has not met before

- My roommate arranged a *blind date* for me so that I'd have someone to go to the party with.
- Sam didn't want to go on a *blind date*, but he actually enjoyed it very much.

fix up (with)   to arrange for two people to date
also: **set up (with)**

GRAMMAR/USAGE NOTES: *Fix up* and *set up* are separable. The subject of the sentence is the person who arranges the date for another person.

- Craig didn't have a date for the dance, so he was glad when his older brother *fixed* him *up.*
- The single mother's sons finally succeeded in *setting* her *up with* a date.

old flame   a previous boyfriend or girlfriend
opposite meaning: **new flame**

- Kim was surprised when she accidentally met an *old flame* at the supermarket.
- Fred's *new flame* has caused him to forget completely about his difficult divorce.

break up (with) to end a relationship, to stop dating
also: **split up (with), break off**
GRAMMAR/USAGE NOTES: *Break off* is separable.
- In the United States, 50 percent of all married people eventually **break up.**
- Dwight **split up with** his wife after ten years of marriage.
- The two high school students were tired of dating each other, so they **broke** their relationship **off.**

stand someone up to fail to appear for a date, to leave waiting, to cancel at the last minute
GRAMMAR NOTE: The idiom is separable, and the object is usually after the verb.
- I can't believe that Lydia **stood** Jake **up** last night without even calling him.
- Juergen waited an hour for his date, but it was obvious that she had **stood** him **up.**

make up (with) to become friendly again after an argument or disagreement
also: **get back together, bury the hatchet**
- After two days of not talking to each other, Casey and Ann **made up.**
- Cindy tried to **make up with** her boyfriend, but he was still too upset.
- When two married people split up, they sometimes **get back together** at a later time.
- Let's **bury the hatchet** and try to fix the problems in our relationship.

EXERCISES

A. Fill in each blank with the missing part of the idiom.

Paul didn't have anyone to accompany him to an important dinner engagement because his date had just stood him _____ . He called
1
a colleague, Rita, who was able to fix him up _____ a friend as
2
a _____ date. Paul was pleasantly surprised to see that the date was Elaine,
3
an old _____ whom he had broken _____ with a couple of years
4   5
earlier but had always wanted to contact again.

In the beginning Elaine didn't want to go _____ with Paul, but he
6
talked about wanting to make up _____ her and about thinking it
7
was possible that they could eventually _____ with each other again.
8
Elaine wasn't sure she believed Paul, but finally she agreed to dine with him.
Their date went very well indeed, and Paul and Elaine are now happy to be going
steady again.

B. Choose the statement in the right column that best responds to each question in the left column. Write the appropriate number in the blank.

NOTE: *To do this as a listening exercise, cover up the left column before you start the tape.*

1. Have you and your girlfriend already buried the hatchet?

2. Did you hear that Mr. and Mrs. Wilson have broken up?

3. Would you like me to set you up with a date for the dance?

4. Do you know why Cynthia stood you up?

5. When did you meet your new flame?

____ a. They split up? I thought that their marriage was strong.

____ b. I don't have any idea. I hope she's not angry at me.

____ c. No, she's not interested in getting back together yet.

____ d. No, I'm not interested in another blind date.

____ e. It was shortly after I'd split up with my old flame.

C. Use the idioms in your spoken or written answers to the following questions.

1. What are some common places to go when you *take* someone *out?*

2. How long should you *go with* someone before you consider marriage?

3. Have you ever *stood* someone *up?* Why? Have you ever been *stood up?*

4. Have you ever gone on a *blind date?* If so, how was it? If not, would you like to? Why or why not?

5. What are some possible reasons why 50 percent of American married couples *split up?* What is the percentage in your country?

D. Using the idioms from this unit, develop a dialogue or role play about your dating situation. You may include the following information:

- whether you're going with one person now, or whether you go out with different people;
- if you're going steady, how long you've been going with this person;
- how often you take someone out, and where you usually go;
- if you've ever made up with someone, and what you did to bury the hatchet;
- whether you've ever been fixed up with a date.

Unit 19
Inviting

How about . . . ?   a question form that is often used to make an invitation

GRAMMAR NOTE: This idiom is usually followed by a gerund (verb + *-ing*) or a noun.

■ Hi, Jane, I'm glad to see you. *How about* going to the dance with me tonight?

■ I have an idea. *How about* lunch and a movie tomorrow afternoon?

be free   to be available for some occasion

■ *Are* you *free* Saturday night to go to the museum reception?

■ I called Tom to see if he *was free* to attend the meeting with me.

ask out   to invite on a date

GRAMMAR NOTE: This idiom is separable.

■ Poor Gary had to *ask out* several women before one of them accepted his invitation to the charity ball.

■ Have you *asked* Jill *out* on a date yet?

have over   to invite someone to visit one's home

GRAMMAR NOTE: This idiom is separable.

■ Christina *had over* her entire family for Christmas dinner.

■ I'd like to *have* you *over* for lunch some day when you're free.

go along (with)   to accompany to a social activity
also: **come along (with), tag along (with)**

■ Wilma *went along with* her friends to the shopping center even though she really didn't want to.

■ Would you like to *come along with* us to Disneyland?

■ Bob let his younger brothers *tag along* to the park because they asked nicely.

take someone up on   to accept an invitation or other offer
also: **You're on**

GRAMMAR NOTES: *Take someone up on* is used with an object that directly follows the verb. *You're on* is a sentence that doesn't change form.

■ When Doris's boyfriend asked her to go with him on an Alaskan cruise, she didn't hesitate to *take* him *up on* it.

■ Did you say you wanted to pay for dinner tonight? *You're on!*

turn down   to refuse an invitation or other offer

GRAMMAR NOTE: This idiom is separable.

- I wouldn't *turn down* anyone who offered me a chance at a million-dollar reward.
- Mr. Greer has asked his neighbor out many times, but she continues to *turn* him *down*.

take a raincheck   to postpone an invitation until a later time

USAGE NOTE: Don't confuse this idiom with the similar one in Unit 15, where it is used for purchasing unavailable sale items at a later date.

- I'm too busy to accept your kind invitation this time, but I'll *take a raincheck*, OK?
- Instead of turning his invitation down right away, she *took a raincheck*.

EXERCISES

A. Fill in each blank with the missing part of the idiom.

1. Anthony had his friends _____ to his house to watch the Super Bowl.

2. When René _____ Suzanne out on a date, she just laughed and walked away.

3. Suzanne shouldn't have acted that way when she _____ René down.

4. I'll have to check my schedule to see if I'm _____ Friday night.

5. How _____ going to the modern art exhibit at the museum?

6. Can I go _____ with you to the beach? I have nothing to do.

7. Oscar _____ his girlfriend up on her offer to pay for dinner.

8. I'd love to go, but I'm too busy this week. Can I take a _____?

B. Choose the statement in the right column that best responds to each question in the left column. Write the appropriate number in the blank.

 NOTE: *To do this as a listening exercise, cover up the left column before you start the tape.*

1. Can my little sister come along with us to the zoo?

2. When Pete asked you out, did you take him up on it?

3. I'd like to have you over for coffee and dessert this weekend, OK?

4. How about renting a video to watch tonight?

5. When will you be free to drive to Los Angeles?

____ a. No, I'm not interested in dating him, so I turned him down.

____ b. I probably can't go with you for a couple of weeks.

____ c. This Saturday would be perfect. You're on!

____ d. I'm sorry. I've got a headache, so I want to go to bed early.

____ e. Sure, she can tag along if you don't mind watching her.

C. Use the idioms in your spoken or written answers to the following questions.

1. If someone invited you to go skydiving (to jump out of an airplane), would you *take* them *up on* it? Why or why not?

2. Who were the last people that you *had over* to your home?

3. Do you think it's a good idea for a woman to *ask* a man *out* on a date? Why or why not?

4. What would you say if you wanted to *turn* someone *down* in a kind way?

5. Discuss various reasons why someone would *take a raincheck.*

D. Using the idioms from this unit, develop a dialogue or role play about inviting friends to do something. You may include the following information:

- what friends you asked to go along with you;
- whether your friends took you up on your suggestion;
- what time you and your friends were free;
- whether any of your friends had to turn you down;
- whether you had your friends over to your place afterwards.

Unit 20
Visiting

pay a visit   to visit (usually by previous arrangement)
also: **call on**

GRAMMAR/USAGE NOTES: These idioms describe more formal visits that are usually prearranged. An object can be put after the verb in *pay a visit.*

- The country doctor *paid a visit* to a sick patient on a distant farm.
- I made sure to *pay* Alexandra *a visit* when I traveled to Chicago.
- The salesman *called on* the manager at the appointed time.

drop in (on)   to visit (usually not by previous arrangement)
also: **drop by, come by, come over**

USAGE NOTE: Only the main entry can be used with *on,* followed by the identity of the person who is visited.

- It's a pleasure to see you again. Please *drop in* any time.
- When Stan *dropped in on* an old friend, she was quite surprised to see him.
- I wanted to *drop by* earlier, but when it got so late I decided not to *come over.*
- Why don't you *come by* tonight and we'll talk some more?

swing by   to visit (often for the purpose of getting or buying something)
also: **stop by**

USAGE NOTE: These forms can also be used for informal visits (see previous entry).

- Why don't you *swing by* my house to borrow the tools that you need?
- Doreen *stopped by* the supermarket on her way home from work.

stop over   to visit (usually overnight)
related form: **stopover** (noun meaning "short stop")

USAGE NOTE: Both idioms usually refer to an airplane trip.

- On our trip north, we *stopped over* in San Francisco for two days.
- The airplane made a *stopover* in New York before continuing to Paris.

get together   to meet or gather for a visit
related form: **get-together** (noun)

USAGE NOTE: This idiom is used for family gatherings and other group visits.

- All of my relatives *get together* at Thanksgiving for a turkey feast.
- If you'd like, we can have a *get-together* this weekend in my backyard.

show in   to guide someone inside, especially into one's home
also: **Come on in**

GRAMMAR NOTE: *Show in* is separable. *Come on in* is an invariable expression.

- Someone is knocking at the door. Could you *show* them *in?*
- Hey, Joe, I'm glad you could make it. *Come on in!*

make oneself at home   to relax by removing one's coat, sitting down, and getting comfortable.

USAGE NOTE: This idiom is used when guests first arrive.

- I'm glad you could come. Please *make yourself at home!*
- Helena's guests *made themselves at home* in her warm and cozy living room.

feel at home   to feel comfortable, to be relaxed

USAGE NOTE: This idiom is often used when it takes some time to feel relaxed in a new environment.

- The Johnsons are good hosts. They know how to make their guests *feel at home.*
- It's difficult to *feel at home* in a foreign country where you don't speak the language.

take a seat   to sit on a couch, chair, stool, or other similar pieces of furniture

- Give me your coat and then *take a seat* in the living room. The meeting will begin soon.

show out   to guide someone out of somewhere such as one's workplace or home
also: **see out**

GRAMMAR NOTE: These idioms are separable.

- The zoo ranger had to *show out* several families that were still in the zoo when it closed.
- It was so nice of you to come. Let me *see* you *out.*

EXERCISES

A.   **Fill in each blank with the missing part of the idiom.**

ANDY: Hi, Julie. I'm glad you decided to drop _____ on me today.

                        1

JULIE: Well, you said you wanted me to _____ you a visit before I

                                    2

returned home, so I decided to swing _____ on my way to the

                                               3

travel agency.

ANDY: Great. Let me _____ you in . . . here's the living room, and the

                                 4

kitchen is over there. Please make yourself at _____ while I get us

                                                 5

some drinks.

JULIE: (Andy returns with sodas) Andy, your new apartment is really wonderful. As

soon as I entered, I _____ right at home.

                              6

ANDY: Isn't it comfortable? It's a perfect place to get _____ with friends.

                                                    7

Why are you standing? Take a _____ on the couch.

                                  8

JULIE: OK. I have to be at the travel agency by 5:00 p.m., though.

ANDY: To get your plane ticket home?

JULIE: Yes. I'm going to stay with my folks a while. Before that, however, I've arranged

      to _____ over in New York on my way.

                  9

ANDY: You've got friends there?

JULIE: Yes. They're going to show me the sights, like the view from the Empire State

      Building.

ANDY: Oh, that reminds me. The view from the roof of this building is pretty good.

      When I show you _____ later, I'll take you up there, OK?

                           10

JULIE: Sounds great to me!

B.   **Choose the statement in the right column that best responds to each question in the left column. Write the appropriate number in the blank.**

NOTE: *To do this as a listening exercise, cover up the left column before you start the tape.*

1. It was nice of you to come tonight. Would you like me to show you out?
2. Hi, Joe. Am I very late?
3. Shouldn't we stop by the store for a few things?
4. Are we flying straight through to Australia in one day?
5. Have Melinda and her new fiancé called on her parents yet?

____ a. Not really. Come on in and take a seat!

____ b. Yes, they finally paid them a visit last week.

____ c. I can see myself out. Thanks for making me feel at home.

____ d. No, we'll make a stopover in Hawaii.

____ e. Yes, we need to swing by for some milk and eggs.

C.   **Use the idioms in your spoken or written answers to the following questions.**

1. How would you *make yourself at home* in a friend's house or apartment?
2. What are some common food items you buy when you *stop by* the store?
3. How often do you *get together* with your best friend? Your parents?
4. Is it polite or impolite to *drop in on* someone without calling first? Why?
5. When was the last time you *paid a visit* to the doctor? What was wrong?

D.   **Using the idioms from this unit, tell a classmate about a party that you invited your friends to. You may include the following information:**

- what friends you invited to your get-together;
- what day and time you told your friends to come over;
- whether you had to swing by the store to buy some last-minute party things;
- whether you showed in your guests or if they showed themselves in;
- how you made your guests feel at home.

Review: Units 11–20

A. Circle the expression that best completes each sentence.

1. Did you review your notes in case there's a _____ in class today?
   a. blind date
   b. crank call
   c. pop quiz

2. Would you please answer the doorbell and _____ the guests?
   a. show in
   b. get back together
   c. drop in on

3. We couldn't finish our meal, so we asked the waitress for a _____.
   a. raincheck
   b. doggy bag
   c. pot luck

4. How about _____ me to the newest exhibit at the art gallery?
   a. showing out
   b. going along with
   c. calling back

5. It was nice to _____ Alexis after all these years of no contact.
   a. hear from
   b. take after
   c. hand down

6. If something seems too expensive, you should _____ further before buying it.
   a. pick up
   b. take back
   c. shop around

7. Arnold shouldn't have _____ school to get a job. He should have graduated first.
   a. broken up with
   b. bought up
   c. dropped out of

8. Mrs. Lee thought that there would be leftovers, but all the food on the table was _____.
   a. eaten up
   b. taken out
   c. eaten in

9. How long has William been _____ Yoshiko? They seem happy together.
   a. fixing up with
   b. going out with
   c. turning down

10. I didn't want to sit next to Dave because I knew that he would _____ with all his crazy theories.
    a. bend my ear
    b. dash off
    c. make up

B. Indicate whether each statement is TRUE (T) or FALSE (F).

_____ 1. You would stock up on items if you decided to go window-shopping.

_____ 2. One way to break the ice is to shake hands with someone you've just met.

_____ 3. When you ask someone to hold on, they're going to return your call.

_____ 4. If someone tells you to take a seat, they're trying to make you feel at home.

_____ 5. A bargain-hunter would pick out the most economical items available.

_____ 6. A teacher's pet might help to hand out papers to the students.

_____ 7. If you're still going out several times a week, it means that you've probably settled down.

_____ 8. If all the food is wolfed down, then some is left over.

_____ 9. You're making small talk if you're shooting the breeze with someone.

_____ 10. Someone who takes you up on your offer is taking a raincheck.

C. Complete the puzzle with the missing parts of the idioms in the sentences below.

ACROSS

2. What a sweet _____ you have!
4. I'll get in _____ with you later.
5. The gang member is a high school _____.
7. I hate listening to _____-yak.
9. You should _____ up on your Spanish before your trip.
11. Let's get _____ for coffee, OK?
12. She went to the library and hit the _____.
13. I've got to go. See you _____.

DOWN

1. The flight made a _____ in Alaska.
3. I love getting a good deal. I'm such a bargain-_____.
6. Should we pay a _____ to your parents?
8. How _____ going to a movie with me?
9. My son is just a chip off the old _____.
10. How long have you been going _____ with Alan?

Unit 21
Health and Exercise

be in shape   to be in good or bad physical condition
opposite meaning: **be out of shape** (to be in poor physical condition)
GRAMMAR/USAGE NOTES: Adjectives such as *good* and *excellent* are often added. This idiom can also be used with the verbs *keep* and *stay*. With adjectives such as *bad* and *terrible*, it has the opposite meaning.

- Mr. Al-Shamsi *is in* excellent *shape* for a sixty-year-old man, but his son Tareq *is in* terrible *shape* for a forty-year-old.
- You look wonderful, Ann. How do you *keep in shape?*
- Maxine has *been out of shape* for years because she never exercises.

be on a diet   to control food consumption in order to lose weight
also: **go on a diet**

- Noreen has *been on a diet* for so long that she hardly remembers when she started.
- I can't put these pants on anymore. It's time to *go on a diet!*

put on weight   to gain weight

- During holiday seasons, many people overeat and *put on weight.*
- I haven't seen Yoko for a long time. I hear that she's really *put on weight.*

warm up   to loosen the body muscles before exercising
also: **limber up**

GRAMMAR/USAGE NOTE: These idioms are separable. Objects such as *body* and *muscles* can be used.

- It's very important to *warm up* before doing physical exercise.
- The gymnast *limbered* his muscles *up* before doing a practice routine.

work out   to do physical exercise, such as lifting weights
also: **get a workout**

- Jeremy goes to the fitness center three times a week to *work out* with a friend.
- Mrs. Lancaster *gets a* good *workout* by taking an aerobics class.

build up   to increase muscle size and strength gradually
GRAMMAR/USAGE NOTES: This idiom is separable. The object can be parts of the body or the word *strength*.

- Lenny is trying to *build up* his shoulders so that he can hit a baseball farther.
- Even older people can *build* their strength *up* by doing simple, regular exercise.

catch one's breath   to stop exercising in order to breathe more normally

USAGE NOTE: This idiom is used when someone has been exercising so much that they are having trouble breathing and need to stop for a moment.

■ One of the soccer players left the field so that she could **catch her breath.**

■ I stopped running for a moment in order to **catch my breath.**

work off   to rid oneself of extra weight or stress

GRAMMAR/USAGE NOTES: This idiom is separable. It is usually used with the objects *weight, stress,* or *tension.*

■ Jeff is so annoyed by the extra weight around his waist that he's decided to **work** it **off.**

■ I find that yardwork is an excellent way of **working off** tension and stress in my life.

lay off   to avoid as a habit, to abstain from

also: **swear off**

USAGE NOTE: These idioms are used with objects such as food items and cigarettes.

■ One of the best ways to lose weight is to **lay off** desserts and other sweet things.

■ When Rudolph reached 300 pounds, he decided to **swear off** snacks.

cool off   to become cool, to lose heat or warmth from the body

also: **cool down**

USAGE NOTE: These idioms are used after one becomes hot and sweaty from exercise. They also apply to the weather (see Unit 10).

■ Stella **cooled off** in the shower after a long game of racquetball.

■ After strenuous activity, it's recommended that the muscles be given time to **cool down.**

EXERCISES

A.   **Fill in each blank with the missing part of the idiom.**

1. Amy had to _____ her breath after climbing the long flight of stairs.

2. The athlete stretched his muscles thoroughly after warming them _____.

3. I can hardly recognize Latka since he put on so much _____.

4. Ursula finds that long-distance running helps her to _____ off job stress.

5. Adel goes to the gym every day to _____ up his muscle strength.

6. I find that it's more fun to work _____ on weight machines with a friend.

7. Mrs. Eagleton didn't eat a piece of pie because she's on a _____.

8. Mr. Proctor is in excellent _____. He looks twenty years younger than he looked before.

9. The boys were hot from playing football, so they sat under a tree to _____ off.

10. Germaine was forced to _____ off all unnecessary sugar while he was on the training program.

B. Choose the statement in the right column that best responds to the question in the left column. Write the appropriate number in the blank.

NOTE: *To do this as a listening exercise, cover up the left column before you start the tape.*

1. We've been jogging for thirty minutes. Don't you need to catch your breath?

2. It smells bad in here! When are you going to lay off cigarettes?

3. How long do you warm up before a serious workout?

4. Have you ever been stronger than you are now?

5. Why are you working out so hard?

____ a. No, I haven't. I've really been building up my strength lately.

____ b. A short rest sounds good. We can cool off under that tree.

____ c. I'm trying to work off the stress of a busy day.

____ d. I take about twenty minutes to limber up all my muscles.

____ e. I've decided to swear off them on my next birthday.

C. Use the idioms in your spoken or written answers to the following questions.

1. What do people do to **build up** their strength?

2. What causes people to **put on weight?** Why might they finally decide to **go on a diet?**

3. For what reasons do people enjoy **working out** at a gym or fitness center?

4. Why is it important to **warm up** before vigorous exercise and to cool down afterwards?

5. What are some ways that people **work off** stress and tension?

D. Using idioms from this unit, develop a dialogue or role play about your own health condition and your present or future exercise program. You may include the following information:

- whether you are in shape or out of shape;
- whether you need to go on a diet;
- what you could do to build up your strength;
- whether you have ever worked out at a gym or fitness center;
- what foods or drinks you would like to swear off;
- what you do to work off stress and tension.

Unit 22
Illness and Disease

be under the weather   not to be feeling well, be sick

USAGE NOTE: The verb *feel* can also be used.

- Jane's head and neck hurt, and her nose is stuffy. She must *be under the weather.*
- I stayed home from school because I *felt under the weather.*

be run-down   to be tired and in poor physical condition

USAGE NOTE: The verb *feel* can also be used. The poor condition usually results from overwork or lack of sleep.

- Stan *was run-down* from working long hours on his research project.
- If you *feel run-down* from lack of sleep, you should get more rest!

feel out of it   to feel strange, not to be in normal condition
also: **not feel oneself (today)**

USAGE NOTE: This idiom is used when someone is not exactly sick, but still doesn't feel normal.

- I don't know what's wrong with me today. I just *feel* completely *out of it.*
- Usually Martha has more energy, but she's just *not feeling herself today.*

come down with   to develop an illness
also: **catch a cold, catch the flu**

- Little Betty *came down with* a cold and had to miss her piano lesson.
- If you don't wear warm clothing to play outside, you'll *catch a cold.*
- I think I *caught the flu* from my girlfriend, who already has it.

run a fever   to have a higher temperature than usual
also: **run a temperature**

- Billy's forehead seems warm to me. I think he's *running a fever.*
- When Darlene caught the flu, she was *running a temperature* of 101 degrees.

go around   to spread from person to person

- Colds and flus tend to *go around* more during the winter months.
- Many employees were sick because the flu was *going around* the office.

run its course   to continue for the expected period of time

- The doctor said there was nothing we could do but let the flu virus *run its course.*
- Even though I took vitamins and rested a lot, my cold *ran its course* for over two weeks.

take a turn for the worse   to become more ill

USAGE NOTE: This idiom is often used for diseases that rapidly become worse. The adjective *sudden* can precede the noun *turn*.

- Even though Mrs. Barton was feeling better, the doctor warned that her cancer was spreading and that soon her condition would *take a turn for the worse.*
- Old Mr. Jenkins seemed to be recovering from his serious illness, but then he *took a* sudden *turn for the worse.*

get a checkup   to visit the doctor for a physical examination

- It is a good idea for older people to *get a checkup* on a yearly basis.
- I haven't been to the doctor to *get a checkup* in over five years.

be laid up   to be forced to rest or to be inactive due to illness or injury
also: **lay up** (active verb form)

GRAMMAR NOTE: This idiom is most often used in the passive form, although the active form, which is separable, can be used to clearly indicate the nature of the illness or injury.

- Judy *was laid up* in bed with the flu on the holiday weekend that she expected to go skiing with her friends.
- Serious injuries from an auto accident *laid* Carl *up* in the hospital for several weeks.

get over   to recover from an illness

- It took Jarek over two weeks to *get over* his deep chest cold.
- If you rest in bed and drink plenty of liquids, you may *get over* the flu more quickly.

EXERCISES

A.   **Fill in each blank with the missing part of the idiom.**

1. Did you touch Willie's forehead? I think he's _____ a fever.

2. I'm sorry I shouted at you. I really _____ out of it today.

3. Do you know that chickenpox is going _____ in the schools?

4. A broken leg laid Brenda _____ in bed for several days.

5. It's amazing how Andy _____ over colds so quickly.

6. Mr. Welton was improving, but then he took a sudden turn for the _____.

7. It's been a long time since I've been to the doctor's office to get a _____.

8. There was nothing that Francine could do about the flu but let it run its _____.

9. Janice can't play tennis today because she's feeling under the _____.

10. My throat hurts and my nose is stuffy. I must be coming _____ with something.

11. Jerome hates the long hours and busy schedule at work, which often make him feel _____-down.

B. Choose the statement in the right column that best responds to the question in the left column. Write the appropriate number in the blank.

NOTE: *To do this as a listening exercise, cover up the left column before you start the tape.*

1. Are you sneezing because you're catching a cold?

2. How long has Cindy been feeling under the weather?

3. Why has Marilyn been laid up in bed for a week?

4. Could you be running a temperature? Your face looks red.

5. Why did Mr. Erickson leave the office early today?

____ a. I hope not. However, I'm not feeling myself today.

____ b. No, I'm not running a fever. I've just been exercising!

____ c. He has to get a checkup for his new insurance policy.

____ d. She's been feeling run-down for a couple of days.

____ e. Her flu took a turn for the worse.

C. Use the idioms in your spoken or written answers to the following questions.

1. What causes people to *come down with* illnesses? Is any illness *going around* right now in your community?

2. How long does it usually take for a cold or flu to *run its course?*

3. What kind of injuries *lay* people *up* in the hospital? Has this ever happened to you?

4. What's the best thing to do if you're *running a fever?*

5. What does the doctor do when you *get a checkup?*

D. Using idioms from this unit, tell a classmate about a past sickness. You may include the following information:

- what illness you came down with;
- whether this illness was going around;
- whether you were running a fever;
- whether you were laid up in bed at any time;
- how long it took you to get over the illness.

Unit 23
Clothing

put on   to wear an item of clothing
also: **have on**

GRAMMAR/USAGE NOTES: These idioms are separable. *Put on* is the action of putting an item of clothing on the body; *have on* is the condition of wearing it.

- How many times have I told you to **put** your jacket **on** before going outside?
- I really like the dress that you **have on**. Where did you get it?

get dressed   to put on all one's usual clothing

- Every morning Hugo takes a shower before he **gets dressed** for work.
- If we don't **get dressed** now, we won't be ready before our guests arrive.

try on   to put on for the purpose of checking size and fit

GRAMMAR/USAGE NOTES: This idiom is separable and is often used when shopping for clothes in a store.

- I'd like to take these dresses into a fitting room and **try** them **on**.
- Why don't you **try on** this old sweater of mine? It might fit you.

dress up   to wear very nice clothing
also: **be (all) decked out**

GRAMMAR NOTE: *Dress up* is often used in passive form.

- Once a month Mr. and Mrs. Jacques **dress up** for a night on the town.
- Why are you **dressed up** so nicely? Do you have a big date?
- Doesn't Talia look lovely? She**'s all decked out** in diamonds and pearls.

go with   to match, to coordinate with

USAGE NOTE: Adverbs such as *well* and *poorly* can be used.

- Do you think that this blouse **goes** well **with** this dress, or should I change?
- Jorge is wearing a silly-looking tie that doesn't **go with** his suit.

take off   to remove one's clothing
also: **peel off, strip off**

USAGE NOTE: The alternate forms are commonly used when someone hurries to remove clothing.

- As soon as I get home, I **take off** my clothes and put on something more comfortable.
- Marvin was so sweaty that he **peeled off** his clothes and jumped into the shower.

fold up   to fold clothing, towels, sheets, and such neatly
>   related idiom: **hang up** (to hang in a closet or on a hook)
>   GRAMMAR NOTE: These idioms are separable.
>   ▪ Mr. Schmidt helped his wife to *fold up* some towels and a large bed sheet.
>   ▪ I've told you not to leave your clothes on the floor. *Hang* them *up* in the closet now.

wear out   to wear until an item of clothing has no further use or value
>   related idiom: **wear through** (to become thin through wear)
>   GRAMMAR NOTE: These idioms are separable and are often used in the passive form.
>   ▪ Children who are physically active tend to *wear* their clothes *out* quickly.
>   ▪ I discarded my favorite pair of jeans because they were *worn through* at the knees.

grow out of   to become too big to wear an item of clothing
>   ▪ As my older son *grows out of* his clothing, we save the best items for his younger brother.
>   ▪ If you buy your daughter a shirt that fits her perfectly now, she'll soon *grow out of* it.

bundle up   to wear warm clothing
>   also: **wrap up**
>   GRAMMAR NOTE: These idioms are separable.
>   ▪ Before we went outside in the freezing weather, we *bundled up.*
>   ▪ It was so cold outside that the mother *wrapped* her baby *up* in a thick blanket.

EXERCISES

A.   **Fill in each blank with the missing part of the idiom.**

MOM: (Holding up blouse in store) Wouldn't this pattern _____ well with

> your skirt? Why don't you put it _____ so we can see how it looks?

BECKY: Good idea. I'll _____ it on in the fitting room.

MOM: Try on this nice skirt too.

BECKY: OK, Mom. My favorite skirt isn't good enough anymore when I need to

> _____ up for a special occasion. It's too _____ out. The

> last time I wanted to wear it, it looked so bad that I had to take it

> _____ and quickly _____ dressed in something else.

MOM: Check that they're one size larger so that you don't grow _____ of

> them quickly. (Pointing to three unfolded blouses) I'll _____ up

> these blouses and put them back on the shelf.

BECKY: The clerk will do that, Mom. You should look for a jacket to _____

> up in on these cold nights.

MOM: No, I'll just fold these blouses up and help you.

BECKY: I guess I'll always be your little girl, Mom!

B. Choose the statement in the right column that best responds to the question in the left column. Write the appropriate number in the blank.

NOTE: *To do this as a listening exercise, cover up the left column before you start the tape.*

1. Why are these pants already worn out? We just bought them for you!

2. Is the baby wrapped up well for the cold weather outside?

3. Do these sandals go well with my bathing suit?

4. Why are you all decked out in your best clothes?

5. What kind of necklace do you have on?

____ a. It's made of pearls. It looks good with my blouse, don't you think?

____ b. Who cares! You'll just be taking them off at the beach.

____ c. I don't know. I guess I wear through clothes quickly!

____ d. I decided to dress up for the piano recital this evening.

____ e. Yes, I've got her bundled up in a warm blanket.

C. Use the idioms in your spoken or written answers to the following questions.

1. For what occasions do people get *dressed up?* What do they wear?

2. What are the reasons for *trying on* clothes before you buy them?

3. Do you *put* pajamas *on* when you go to bed? If not, what do you *put on?*

4. What do people do with clothes they've *grown out of?* What would you do?

5. What laundry do you *fold up* after it's been washed, and what do you *hang up* in the closet?

D. Using idioms from this unit, develop a dialogue or role play about your clothing routine. You may include the following information:

- what you usually put on when you get dressed in the morning;
- whether you wear clothes that are worn out, or whether you replace them immediately;
- what kinds of clothes you try on when you shop at stores;
- what you bundle up in when the weather becomes cold;
- how often you dress up, and what you usually put on.

Unit 24
Budget and Cost

be broke   to have no money
- Could you lend me a few dollars until next week? I'*m broke.*

make ends meet   to live reasonably well without getting into debt
- Every month we have to plan our budget carefully in order to *make ends meet.*
- The Masons couldn't *make ends meet*, so they had to declare bankruptcy.

get by   to manage to survive on limited resources
also: **make do (on)**
USAGE NOTE: These idioms are used when someone doesn't make or have enough money to live comfortably.
- How can you and your large family *get by* on such a limited income?
- Mr. Otto had to *make do on* a small pension after he retired.

cut corners   to save money by economizing
DEFINITION NOTE: Economizing involves buying the cheapest possible items and using as little as possible at one time.
- The only way that we're able to make ends meet is by *cutting corners* wherever possible.
- Sometimes when a company *cuts corners*, the quality of its products suffers.

do without   to live or survive without something
- Bob had to *do without* a car in college because he couldn't afford to buy one.
- Even though our food budget is limited, there's no way I can *do without* dessert.

come to   to total, to amount to
USAGE NOTE: This idiom is used when paying for several items or services at one time.
- The total cost of repairs on Kathy's car *came to* $750.
- Sir, your grocery bill *comes to* $42.95.

pick up the tab   to pay for the cost of something, often a meal
also: **foot the bill, be on someone**
- The salesperson *picked up the tab* when she invited the executive to lunch.
- Our company *foots the bill* for the annual Christmas party.
- Don't worry about the price of your meal. It*'s on me!*

73

be a steal   to be very cheap
>   related idiom: **for a song** (for little money)
>   ■ This late-model used car is in excellent condition with low mileage. It*'s a steal*
>   at $3,000!
>   ■ I was happy when I bought a dining table and four chairs at the garage sale
>   *for a song.*

cost an arm and a leg   to be very expensive
>   related idiom: **pay through the nose** (to pay too much for something)
>   ■ It *costs an arm and a leg* to visit the doctor if you don't have medical insurance.
>   ■ I had to *pay through the nose* to get my car repaired at a service station in the middle
>   of the desert.

be a rip-off   to be too expensive
>   also: **be highway robbery**
>   ■ You shouldn't shop at that store because the prices *are a rip-off.*
>   ■ Are you telling me that the cheapest rooms in this hotel cost $200 a night?
>   That*'s highway robbery!*

EXERCISES

A.   **Fill in each blank with the missing part of the idiom.**

1. That camera costs an arm and a _____ in this store. You can get it much
   cheaper elsewhere.

2. Forty-five dollars for an oil change? What a _____-off!

3. The salesperson picked up the _____ for the business lunch.

4. Sir, your total _____ to $62.65. Would you like a receipt?

5. The apartment residents had to do _____ water for two days because the
   main pipe had broken.

6. How does Kimberley make ends _____ with three kids and a part-time job?

7. Do you have an extra $10 that you can lend me? I'm completely _____.

8. If you wait to buy this ski equipment on sale in the springtime, it will be a real
   _____.

9. The Adams family learned to cut _____ when Mr. Adams lost his job.

10. Mrs. Stearns was able to _____ by on the small income from her
    retirement annuity.

B. Choose the statement in the right column that best responds to the question in the left column. Write the appropriate number in the blank.

NOTE: *To do this as a listening exercise, cover up the left column before you start the tape.*

1. Doesn't it cost an arm and a leg for Linda to attend a private college?	___ a. Sorry, I don't have any money either.
2. Can I pick up the tab for lunch? You paid last time.	___ b. Are you kidding? I think you paid through the nose for it.
3. Could I borrow some money for the movie? I'm broke until next week.	___ c. There's only one way—we've got to cut corners everywhere.
4. Wasn't this coffeemaker a steal at $165?	___ d. It does, but her grandparents are footing the bill.
5. How can we go to Europe if the cost would probably come to $4,000?	___ e. I'd never let you pay. Of course the meal is on me.

C. Use the idioms in your spoken or written answers to the following questions.

1. What might the bill for four people at an expensive restaurant *come to?*
2. What might you have to *do without* if you lived in the isolated desert?
3. Most people lose money gambling in Las Vegas, so *is* it *a rip-off?* Why or why not?
4. What are some ways that people *make ends meet?*
5. For what reasons do some people have to *get by* on almost no money? Why do some people choose to live in this way?

D. Using idioms from this unit, develop a dialogue or role play about your real or imagined financial problems. You may include the following information:

- how much money you could make do on each week;
- what your average food bill comes to;
- whether or not you have to struggle to make ends meet;
- ways that you cut corners;
- something you bought that you paid through the nose for;
- extra things in life that you sometimes have to do without.

Unit 25
Time

in a while   after a short period of time
also: **after a while**

USAGE NOTE: Adjectives such as *little* and *short* can be used.

- Diego said that he was almost done with his homework and could go outside to play *in a* little *while.*
- Mrs. Felton was complaining about a headache, but *after a while* it disappeared.

for a while   for a short period of time

USAGE NOTE: Adjectives such as *little* and *short* can be used, and *for* can be removed.

- I'm somewhat in a hurry, but I can visit *for a* little *while.*
- This morning it snowed *a* short *while* before the sun appeared.

for the time being   temporarily
also: **for now**

- We'll have to keep our old car *for the time being* until we can afford to buy a new one.
- Even though Jung-Jae is very unhappy with conditions at his job, he has to continue working there *for now.*

for good   permanently, forever
also: **for keeps**

USAGE NOTE: *For keeps* is more informal than *for good.*

- Mrs. Wilcox has left her unfaithful husband *for good* and will soon file for a divorce.
- Deirdre wants to stop drinking coffee *for keeps* because she thinks it's bad for her health.

from now on   now and into the future
also: **once and for all**

USAGE NOTE: The related form *once and for all* includes the idea that someone has finally decided to take action.

- Allen has lost fifty pounds and plans to control his weight *from now on.*
- After years of quitting cigarettes and starting again, Lita decided to stop *once and for all.*

sooner or later   eventually, at some future time

    also: **one of these days**

    USAGE NOTE: These idioms involve the idea that some action or situation is inevitable in the future.

- It seems like it's been raining for days, but it'll stop **sooner or later.**
- **One of these days** I want to take a trip to Canada, but I don't know when I'll have the time.

from time to time   occasionally, sometimes

    also: **every so often, once in a while**

- **From time to time** wild animals come into our backyard searching for food.
- **Every so often** I forget to call my parents on Sunday evening.
- **Once in a while** Bernice likes to sleep late in the morning.

over and over (again)   repeatedly

    also: **time and time again, time after time**

- Jim likes that new jazz CD so much that he can listen to it **over and over again.**
- The baby tried to climb up in the chair **time and time again.**
- I've told you **time after time** not to run into the street without looking both ways!

day in and day out   continuously for a period of days

    related idiom: **around the clock** (twenty-four hours a day)

- Mrs. Burns is tired of staying at home **day in and day out.** She's ready to look for a job.
- City crews worked **around the clock** to repair the damage from the earthquake.

in time (to)   before the appointed time (to do something)

    related idiom: **on time** (exactly at the appointed time, punctually)

    USAGE NOTE: These idioms are very similar in meaning. *In time* provides the idea that it might be too late to do something after the appointed time.

- The Varricks left for the lecture early so they'd arrive **in time to** get good seats.
- Frances thought she'd be late to class, but she managed to get there **on time.**

EXERCISES

A.   **Fill in each blank with the missing part of the idiom.**

1. For the time _____, Kim has no intention of selling her condominium.

2. Sooner or _____ we all have to decide what we want to do in life.

3. I like to get away from everyone and be alone from _____ to time.

4. Our neighbor's dog barks _____ in and day out. Doesn't it ever get tired?

5. From _____ on I promise to save more time to be with you and the children.

6. Carlos heard a strange ringing sound in his ear for a _____.

7. _____ a short while, the ringing in his ear stopped.

8. George tried to reach Helena over and _____, but there was no answer.

9. Soon I'm going to lose all this extra weight _____ good.

10. Mr. Martinez rushed to the station but didn't get there in _____ to catch his train.

B. Choose the statement in the right column that best responds to the question in the left column. Write the appropriate number in the blank.

NOTE: *To do this as a listening exercise, cover up the left column before you start the tape.*

1. Do you think that Arnold will ever move back to the city?	____ a. I'm not hungry for now. I'll have something after a while.
2. Would you like a snack now, or would you prefer to wait for a while?	____ b. Yes, I do, but at least I don't have one now.
3. Do you ever feel the need to eat junk food anymore?	____ c. No, I think he'll live in the country from now on.
4. Do you still get headaches every so often?	____ d. Most of them are, but once in a while one of them is late.
5. Are your employees always on time to work?	____ e. No, I've stopped that habit once and for all.

C. Use the idioms in your spoken or written answers to the following questions.

1. Are there any stores in your neighborhood that are open *around the clock?* What kind of stores?

2. Is there any favorite place that you visit *time after time?* Describe the place.

3. Name something unusual or interesting you'd like to do *one of these days.*

4. Is there a bad habit that you've already quit *for good?* Is there any other bad habit that you'd like to quit *once and for all?*

5. *For the time being*, what is your main goal in life?

D. Using idioms from this unit, develop a dialogue or role play involving your life situation at this time. You may include the following information:

- which family members or friends you are living with for now;
- which family members or friends you see day in and day out, and which you see only every so often;
- where you go from time to time to relax and be alone;
- what promises you'd like to keep from now on;
- whether you are happy with your life for the time being.

Unit 26
Movement and Position

stand up   to rise from a sitting or lying position; to be standing
- When the president of the United States entered the room, everyone *stood up* out of respect.
- There were so many passengers on the bus that I had to *stand up* in the aisle.

sit up   to sit erect (with a straight back)
related idiom: **sit down** (to be seated)

USAGE NOTE: *Sit up* is often used as a command when someone is slouching (sitting with a curved back). The adjective *straight* can be added.
- How many times have I told you not to slouch in your chair? *Sit up* straight!
- All the students *sat down* when the teacher entered the classroom.

make room for   to create space for
- Normally only five people can fit comfortably into Samir's car, but when necessary he can *make room fo*r six or seven.
- I don't see how we're going to *make room for* a TV and stereo in our crowded bedroom.

move over   to shift one's position to the left or right
USAGE NOTE: This idiom is used when space is needed for someone or something else.
- Can you *move over* so I can sit on the sofa too?
- The students in the front row had to *move over* to make room for another desk chair.

take up   to occupy
USAGE NOTE: This idiom is used with objects such as *space* and *room*. Additional words such as a *lot of* and *too much* can be added.
- The new file cabinet Helen bought for her office *takes up* a lot of room.
- I couldn't sit on the couch because my friends were *taking up* too much space.

head for   to travel toward a place, to have as a destination
- On very hot days thousands of people *head for* the beach.
- Let's *head for* the sports bar to watch the football game on big-screen TV.

turn back   to return to where someone started traveling from
also: **head back**

- Ten minutes after leaving home, Debbie realized she'd forgotten her glasses and had to *turn back.*
- When the mountain trail became very faint and narrow, we *headed back* to camp.

pass by   to go near or past a place
related form: **passer-by** (noun)

GRAMMAR NOTE: The plural form of the noun is *passers-by.*

- The next time you *pass by* our street, why don't you stop and visit?
- The beautiful window display in the store attracted the attention of *passers-by.*

on foot   by walking

USAGE NOTE: This idiom is often used with the verb *walk*, even though the same meaning is repeated.

- Rain or shine, Gary goes to work and back *on foot* every day.
- When Gloria's bicycle tire went flat, she had to travel the rest of the way *on foot.*

be (right) under someone's nose   to be in an obvious place
also: **stare someone (right) in the face**

- Omar looked everywhere for his wallet, and there it *was right under his nose* on the kitchen counter.
- Aaron is terrible about misplacing things. Even when they're *staring him in the face*, he can't find them.

high and low   everywhere, in every place

USAGE NOTE: This idiom is usually used to describe looking for something whose location is unknown.

- Inez looked *high and low* for her car keys but she couldn't find them.
- The rescuers searched *high and low* for the lost child in the mountains.

EXERCISES

A.   **Fill in each blank with the missing part of the idiom.**

DAVE: (Sitting on a bench at a bus stop with his older brother, Ray) You should ask

the next person who passes _____ how far the beach is from here.

1

RAY: Me? It was your idea to head _____ the beach on _____.

2   3

DAVE: What else could we do? We looked high and _____ for your car keys

4

and never found them.

RAY: Yeah, but at least I found my wallet.

DAVE: Don't remind me—after ten minutes of looking, it was right under your

_____.

5

RAY: Well, what do you want to do—continue, or turn _____?

6

DAVE: Let's just rest here for a while . . . could you _____ over a little? You're

7

taking _____ too much space on the bench.

8

Ray: Oh, right, I make _____ for you and then there isn't enough for me.
₉

Dave: At least could you _____ up straight instead of leaning my way?
₁₀

Ray: I have a better idea—why don't we take this bus?

Dave: It looks crowded. We might have to _____ up.
₁₁

Ray: That's OK with me. Anything's better than more walking!

B. Choose the statement in the right column that best responds to the question in the left column. Write the appropriate number in the blank.

NOTE: *To do this as a listening exercise, cover up the left column before you start the tape.*

1. I've looked high and low for my slippers. Have you seen them?

2. Don't you know that it's bad for your back to slouch in the chair like that?

3. Why did Scott head for the kitchen when we got home?

4. Why did everyone in the courtroom suddenly stand up?

5. Would you mind moving over to make room for me?

____ a. The judge just entered. It's OK to sit down now.

____ b. You're not serious, are you? They're right under your nose!

____ c. He was hungry so he went to get a snack.

____ d. I know, but it's too tiring to sit up straight all the time.

____ e. Of course not. I'm sorry I'm taking up so much space.

C. Use the idioms in your spoken or written answers to the following questions.

1. What are some typical things that you sometimes can't find but later you discover to be *staring you in the face?*

2. Why do *passers-by* slow down or stop to look at an accident? Do you do this?

3. For what reasons might someone have to *turn back* from a trip and go home? Has this ever happened to you?

4. What are some jobs where you would have to *stand up* a lot? Would you mind doing this?

5. Where are some places that you go *on foot* from your house or apartment?

D. Using idioms from this unit, tell a classmate about a time you had to return home because you forgot something. You may include the following information:

- where you were headed for;
- whether you were going there on foot, by bus, and so on;
- at what point you realized you'd forgotten something and headed back home;
- whether you had to look high and low for this thing;
- whether it was right under your nose when you finally found it.

Unit 27
Departing

be off   to be leaving, to leave on one's way to some place
   also: **be out of here**

   USAGE NOTE: These idioms are used only at the moment of leaving, and the subject is usually the first-person pronoun *I* or *we*. The alternate form is informal, and the words *out of* are usually pronounced (and sometimes written) as *outta*.

   ■ Nate, we'**re off**. See you next week.
   ■ I've got only five minutes to get back to the office. I'**m out of here!**
   ■ Sorry I can't stay longer, but I'**m outta here.**

take off   to leave
   also: **hit the road**

   USAGE NOTE: These idioms are used at the moment of leaving and often with expressions such as *It's time to . . .* and *I've got to . . . .* The alternate form is informal.

   ■ Alanna planned to **take off** around nine o'clock, but she didn't actually leave until eleven.
   ■ I didn't realize it was already so late. It's time to **hit the road.**

get going   to start to leave
   USAGE NOTE: This idiom is used when someone needs to get ready to leave.

   ■ I could sit here and talk with you a lot longer, but unfortunately I've got to **get going.**
   ■ If we don't **get going** now, we're going to be late.

head out   to start to leave on a trip
   ■ We set the alarm for 5:00 A.M. so that we could **head out** for the lake early.
   ■ What time are we going to **head out** in the morning?

head off   to go in a certain direction
   ■ Sorry, Mr. Evans, Mike just left. I think he **headed off** in that direction.
   ■ Sally and Todd said good-bye to their mother and **headed off** to school.

dash off   to leave in a hurry
   ■ Do you have to **dash off** already? You just got here a few minutes ago!
   ■ Adel had to **dash off** in order to get home before his parents.

clear out   to leave immediately, to evacuate

     USAGE NOTE: This idiom is often used when a dangerous situation exists.

- Whenever the fire alarm sounds in the building, everyone is expected to **clear out.**
- The police advised residents to **clear out** of town before the hurricane hit.

be long gone   to have already left

- You could have come over much earlier, because my parents **are long gone.**
- Heavy traffic made us late to the airport, and of course our plane **was long gone.**

sneak off   to leave quietly without attracting the attention of others

- Parents have to be careful when small children **sneak off** and do dangerous things like play with matches.
- You mean that Beverly has already left the party? She must have **sneaked off** with her boyfriend!

EXERCISES

A.   **Fill in each blank with the missing part of the idiom.**

1. When Mrs. Kimble leaves work at the end of the day, she likes to announce to everyone, "I'm _____!"

2. If we don't _____ going soon, we'll arrive after dinner has been served.

3. I think I saw Margit head _____ toward her friend's house.

4. I ran outside to find Dana, but he was already long _____.

5. When my friends asked me to stay later, I apologized for having to take _____.

6. The small children had found some scissors and were just starting to _____ off quietly with them when their mother noticed.

7. The children were eager to _____ off from school as soon as classes ended on Friday afternoon.

8. The gang quickly cleared _____ of the public park when they saw a police car approach.

9. We had planned to hit the road by 4:00 A.M., but we didn't finally _____ out until 6:00.

B.   **Choose the statement in the right column that best responds to the question in the left column. Write the appropriate number in the blank.**

     NOTE: *To do this as a listening exercise, cover up the left column before you start the tape.*

1. Has Anthony taken off yet? I need to talk to him.

2. Do you know where Emma dashed off to?

3. What's the matter, Officer?

4. It's really quite late. Shouldn't we hit the road?

5. Why do you have to take off already? The party's just starting!

___ a. I'm sorry, but I have to get going. My baby-sitter is waiting.

___ b. Everyone has to clear out of this area. There's a gas leak.

___ c. Sorry, he's long gone.

___ d. No, not yet. We can wait another half hour.

___ e. I think she headed off in the direction of the delicatessen.

C. Use the idioms in your spoken or written answers to the following questions.

1. Why do young people *sneak off* and do things that their parents don't approve of? What are some of these things?
2. What are some reasons to *head out* early on a driving trip?
3. When was the last time that you had to *dash off* because you were late?
4. When do most people in your country *take off* from work at the end of the day?
5. Do you know the proper way to *clear out* of a building when there's a fire?

D. Using idioms from this unit, develop a dialogue or role play about getting ready to leave for work or school in the morning. You may include the following information:

- at what time you take off in the morning;
- whether you have to sneak off quietly so you don't disturb someone else;
- whether you often have to dash off, or whether you allow enough time to get going;
- in which direction you head off;
- at what time you're off work or school.

Unit 28
Making Things Work

turn on   to cause to function

opposite meaning: **turn off, shut off** (to cause to stop functioning)

GRAMMAR/USAGE NOTES: These idioms are separable. They are commonly used for adjusting water, light, sound, or mechanical equipment.

- Could you **turn on** the water faucet while I hold the end of the hose?
- Please remember to **turn** the light **off** when you're finished in the bathroom.
- It's better to **shut off** a car engine than to let it idle for a long time.

turn up   to increase the force, volume, or brightness

opposite meaning: **turn down** (to decrease the volume or brightness)

GRAMMAR/USAGE NOTES: These idioms are separable. They are commonly used for adjusting water, sound, or lights that can be dimmed.

- **Turn up** the water so that no soap stays on the dishes.
- Vanna **turned up** the stereo when she heard her favorite song.
- It's too bright in here. Please **turn down** the lights halfway.

act up   to function poorly, to malfunction

- The computer is **acting up** again. Sometimes the screen suddenly freezes.
- Whenever the heater in my room **acts up**, I give it a kick and it starts working again.

break down   to stop functioning

- Several people got stuck in the elevator when it **broke down** between floors.
- I called a tow truck when my car **broke down** in the middle of the highway.

burn out   to stop functioning due to extended use

USAGE NOTE: This idiom is commonly used for lightbulbs and other electrical equipment.

- These lightbulbs are designed to last several hundred hours before they **burn out**.
- The supervisor thinks that our copy machine **burned out** due to overuse.

fall apart   to separate into pieces

also: **come apart**

USAGE NOTE: *Fall apart* is used when something is not intended to separate into pieces. *Come apart* is used for this meaning, but also when something is built to be separated.

- The child was so rough playing with her doll that it soon **fell apart**.
- One nice feature of the barbecue set is that it **comes apart** for easy cleaning.

fall off   to separate or detach, to be removed
also: **come off**

GRAMMAR/USAGE NOTES: These idioms may be used with or without an object, but are not separable. They are used for a single piece that separates from a larger part.

- The handle **fell off** the door of the abandoned farmhouse when I pulled on it.
- Is this piece of the radio supposed to **come off** or did I just break it?

out of order   not functioning properly

- The toilets in this restroom are **out of order**. Please use the ones on the next floor.
- If the phone is **out of order**, how are we supposed to contact Carolyn?

be up and running   to be functioning properly again

- The service technician just said that our fax machine would **be up and running** shortly.
- All the office workers were relieved when the computer system **was up and running** again.

EXERCISES

A.   Fill in each blank with the missing part of the idiom.

I work in an office where the machines are always breaking _____
                                                              1
and where "Out of _____" signs are everywhere. In fact, it is very rare
                   2
for all the equipment to be up and _____ at one time.
                                   3
Recently the copy machine has been acting _____ again. You can
                                          4
_____ it on and make a few copies, but then the copies become too
5
light to read. There is no way to turn _____ the darkness level
                                                6
because the button for this function has fallen _____.
                                                7
When you then consider how many lightbulbs are _____ out in
                                                8
various rooms and how many pieces of furniture are falling _____,
                                                            9
you might say I should find a new place to work!

B.   Choose the statement in the right column that best responds to the question in the left column. Write the appropriate number in the blank.

NOTE: *To do this as a listening exercise, cover up the left column before you start the tape.*

1. What's wrong with the lightbulb in the study room?	____ a. Yes, and it's been on long enough. I've got to turn it off.
2. How long will the fax machine be out of order?	____ b. I'm sorry. I'll turn it down.
3. Did you turn on the water for the lawn?	____ c. Yes, it should because it's made to come apart.
4. Why are you playing your music so loudly?	____ d. I think it probably burned out.
5. Will this bookcase fit through our front door?	____ e. It should be up and running very shortly.

C. Use the idioms in your spoken or written answers to the following questions.

1. How could you know that an engine is *acting up?*
2. What would you do if your car *broke down* on the highway?
3. Should you *turn off* all the lights when you leave your home at night? Why or why not?
4. What parts of objects typically *fall off?* What can you do when this happens?
5. It is also possible to talk about people *burning out.* What do you think this means?

D. Using idioms from this unit, develop a dialogue or role play about problems with things around your house or apartment. You may include the following information:

- whether anything is completely out of order;
- whether anything is just acting up;
- whether anything is starting to fall apart;
- whether any lightbulbs have burned out;
- whether it's impossible to turn something on or off, or turn something up or down.

Unit 29
Events

take place   to occur, to happen
- The awards ceremony *took place* in the downtown Civic Auditorium.
- Do you have any idea when the next meeting is *taking place?*
- Is the party going to *take place* at your home or Nick's?

come up   to occur in the future
USAGE NOTE: This idiom usually refers to events in the near future.
- Gertrude's birthday is *coming up* next week. I have to buy her a card and gift.
- The Teasleys discussed what to do on their anniversary *coming up* soon.

go off   to happen according to a plan
also: **come off**
USAGE NOTE: These idioms are often followed by the expression *as planned* or adverbs such as *well*.
- Were there some problems with the conference, or did it *go off* as planned?
- Mrs. Garrett was quite pleased when the charity event *came off* well.

fall through   to fail to happen
USAGE NOTE: The subject of this idiom is very often the word *plan*.
- Jerry will be very disappointed if his vacation plans *fall through* again.
- Plans for the merger *fell through* when company representatives couldn't reach a final agreement.

turn out (for)   to attend, to appear
related form: **turnout** (noun)
- Only a few people *turned out for* the rally organized by the little-known politician.
- Can you believe the *turnout* for the concert? I didn't think the band was that popular!

sell out   to sell all available tickets to an event
related form: **sold-out** (adjective)
GRAMMAR/USAGE NOTES: This idiom is often used in the passive form. Adverbs such as *completely* can be used.
- We may have to schedule another performance if this one *sells out*.
- I'm sorry. The next show is completely *sold out*.
- We waited too long to buy tickets to the *sold-out* play.

be a full house   to be so crowded that there is not enough space

- Because there **was a full house**, people had to stand in the back of the room.
- I'm very sorry, but it**'s a full house**, so you'll have to wait for the next seating.

turn away   not to allow to enter

GRAMMAR/USAGE NOTES: This idiom is separable. It is used when a place is too full to permit more people to enter.

- The concert organizers didn't want to **turn** anyone **away**, but they had no choice because of the full house.
- Several hundred angry people were **turned away** from the sold-out sports event.

rain out   to cancel an event due to rainy weather

USAGE NOTE: This idiom is often used in the passive form.

- The bad storm **rained out** several outdoor events in the city this past weekend.
- The picnic that was **rained out** yesterday has been rescheduled for next Saturday.

ring in the New Year   to celebrate the arrival of the New Year on December 31 and January 1

- Most people like to stay up on New Year's Eve to **ring in the New Year.**
- We **rang in the New Year** by flying to New York and joining the crowd in Times Square.

EXERCISES

A.   **Fill in each blank with the missing part of the idiom.**

1. The surprise birthday party for Tomomi went _____ perfectly. She had no idea that anything had been planned.

2. Don't forget that Mother's Day is _____ up next week, and you have to get a card.

3. Over 2,000 people _____ out for the benefit event for cancer patients.

4. No more tickets to the circus are available because all shows are _____ out.

5. Bad weather never _____ out football or soccer games. Play continues no matter what happens.

6. The stamp convention took _____ in the new conference center.

7. Everyone was disappointed when plans for the school talent show _____ through.

8. The popular nightclub had to turn _____ a long line of people hoping to enter.

9. Watching fireworks is one way that people like to _____ in the New Year.

10. There was a full _____ in the school auditorium for the meeting of the Parent-Teacher Association.

B.   Choose the statement in the right column that best responds to the question in the left column. Write the appropriate number in the blank.

NOTE: *To do this as a listening exercise, cover up the left column before you start the tape.*

1. What are you going to do to ring in the New Year?	____ a. No, there was a full house, so we were turned away.
2. Were you able to attend the lecture last night?	____ b. Oh, I forgot that New Year's Eve is coming up next week.
3. How long did it take for the rock concert to sell out?	____ c. I thought that it went off very well.
4. What was the turnout for the Easter Parade?	____ d. It was completely sold out in only five hours.
5. How did your speech in front of the class come off?	____ e. I heard that about 50,000 people turned out to watch.

C.   Use the idioms in your spoken or written answers to the following questions.

1. When does the next major holiday in your country *take place?* What do people do to celebrate?
2. Is your birthday *coming up* soon? If so, when?
3. Suggest some reasons why vacation plans might *fall through.*
4. Try to think of something you planned that didn't *go off* well. What happened?
5. Can you think of any reason why baseball games can be *rained out*, but not football or soccer games?

D.   Using idioms from this unit, develop a presentation about an important work event or group activity that you planned or helped to plan. You may include the following information:

- when the event or activity took place;
- how many people turned out for the event or activity;
- whether any part of the activity or event fell through;
- whether anyone had to be turned away;
- whether the event or activity went off as you planned;
- whether a similar event is coming up in the future.

Unit 30
Participation and Involvement

take part in   to participate in, to be involved in
also: **be in on**

- Are you going to *take part in* the talent show at school?
- Curtis is the type of manager who wants to *be in on* all important decision-making.

count in   to include, to be part of
opposite meaning: **count out** (not to include)

GRAMMAR/USAGE NOTES: These idioms must be separated, and the object follows the verb.

- If you're planning a trip to Disneyland, please be sure to *count* us *in*.
- Frieda has no interest in joining the union at work, and wants us to *count* her *out*.

have a hand in   to have an active role in
also: **play a part in, play a role in**

USAGE NOTE: Adjectives such as *important* or *key* can be added to the alternate forms.

- You can tell that Beatrice *had a hand in* organizing the social event. Everything was planned perfectly.
- The marriage counselor *played an* important *part in* bringing Stan and his wife together again.
- The president's advisors *play a* key *role in* keeping him informed of the latest international developments.

team up (with)   to work together with, to join or unite
also: **hook up (with)**

- The local police and the FBI *teamed up* to solve the kidnapping case.
- After graduating, Yasmin *hooked up with* several engineers to start her own business.

show up   to appear, to attend, to be present
opposite meaning: **no-show** (someone who doesn't appear)

- If Manuel doesn't *show up* soon, we'll have to leave without him.
- The ticket agent said that the plane was full, but we were able to get seats because there were several *no-shows*.

91

look on   to be a spectator, to watch
related form: **onlooker** (noun)
- Because of her injury, Samantha could only **look on** as her team lost the match.
- Hundreds of **onlookers** saw the small plane fall from the sky and crash.

be left out   not to be included
USAGE NOTE: The verb *feel* can also be used.
- Annette was upset that she **was left out** of her friends' plan to have a party.
- Jason's younger brother **feels left out** when Jason's friends come over to play.

sit out   not to participate
USAGE NOTE: This idiom is often used when someone is unable to participate in a sport or political event.
- A red card in soccer means that a player is ejected and also has to **sit out** the next game.
- The politician has decided to **sit out** the next election due to health reasons.

EXERCISES

A.   Fill in each blank with the missing part of the idiom.

JAN: Thanks for agreeing to take _____ in planning the wedding reception.
                                    1

WES: You can always _____ me in on wedding plans. In fact, so far I've had a
                        2
_____ in all the weddings that my friends have had.
       3

JAN: That's very gracious of you, Wes.

WES: Gracious? I don't know. Maybe it's just because I feel like . . . like someone who

is destined to _____ out the game of love!
                4

JAN: What a strange way to say it. Do you feel left _____ because you don't
                                                       5
have anyone who loves you right now?

WES: You could say that. All my friends have found a partner to _____ up
                                                                   6
with, but I just get to look _____.
                             7

JAN: Wes, you can't be serious. You're a fine person, and someday the right person

will _____ up in your life.
     8

WES: I hope you're right!

B. Choose the statement in the right column that best responds to the question in the left column. Write the appropriate number in the blank.

NOTE: *To do this as a listening exercise, cover up the left column before you start the tape.*

1. Who did you team up with on the advertising campaign?

2. Do you think that bad weather played a part in the plane crash?

3. Can we count you in on a visit to the opera this weekend?

4. Were you in on the decision to fire half of the office workers?

5. Is there any chance we can get a room even though the hotel is booked up?

____ a. No, you can definitely count me out! I hate opera.

____ b. No, I'm glad to say that I didn't take part in that decision.

____ c. We hooked up with the firm of Lambert and Mason.

____ d. Maybe. The clerk said there might be some no-shows.

____ e. I heard that heavy rain might have played a role.

C. Use the idioms in your spoken or written answers to the following questions.

1. For what reasons might someone have to *sit out* a game or other activity? Has this ever happened to you? Why?

2. Why do some people prefer only to *look on* while others are doing sports activities?

3. What are the advantages and disadvantages of *teaming up with* friends to travel together?

4. For what reasons might someone *be left out* of an activity? Has this ever happened to you? Why?

5. How do people *take part in* politics? Are you an active citizen of your country? Why or why not?

D. Using idioms from this unit, tell a classmate about your involvement in an activity related to work, school, or home. You may include the following information:

- what activity you had a hand in;
- whether you teamed up with someone else;
- how many people showed up for the activity;
- whether each person took part in the activity, or whether some just looked on;
- whether anyone felt left out.

Review: Units 21–30

A. Circle the expression that best completes each sentence.

1. The wedding will _____ on Sunday, May 1, on the south lawn of Balboa Park.
   a. turn out
   b. fall through
   c. take place

2. Jim wants to lose weight, so he's going to _____ sweets and snacks.
   a. lay off
   b. grow out of
   c. build up

3. After you _____ your clothes, be sure to hang them up in the closet.
   a. take off
   b. put on
   c. do without

4. James has finally decided to quit smoking _____. His plan is to stop on his anniversary.
   a. from time to time
   b. for good
   c. time and time again

5. I was sorry to hear that your son has _____ a serious case of the measles.
   a. showed out
   b. passed by
   c. come down with

6. You paid only $5 for this bicycle? That certainly _____.
   a. is a steal
   b. costs an arm and a leg
   c. gets by

7. Don't worry about the bill. I'll _____.
   a. make ends meet
   b. be in shape
   c. pick up the tab

8. We looked _____ for the missing sunglasses, but we never found them.
   a. for good
   b. high and low
   c. on time

9. The new queen-sized bed _____ too much space in our small bedroom.
   a. takes up
   b. cuts corners with
   c. tries on

10. Oh, no, I hear strange noises from the engine. It's _____ again.
    a. up and running
    b. acting up
    c. worn through

B. Indicate whether each statement is TRUE (T) or FALSE (F).

_____ 1. You might dress up to go to a party ringing in the New Year.

_____ 2. If an event comes off well, then it falls through.

_____ 3. Something can break down by falling apart.

_____ 4. You should get a strong workout before you warm up.

_____ 5. If you had a hand in something, then you'd be left out.

_____ 6. A player feeling out of it might choose to sit out a game.

_____ 7. You'd bundle up if you wanted to cool off.

_____ 8. If you're run-down day in and day out, then you're probably out of shape.

_____ 9. If your clothes are worn out, then you're trying them on for the first time.

_____ 10. You might move over to make room for someone who wants to take a seat.

C. Complete the puzzle with the missing parts of the idioms in the sentences below.

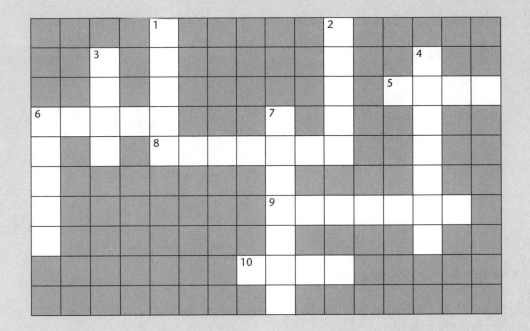

ACROSS

5. Did Ann _____ up on time?
6. Can I borrow a dollar? I'm _____.
8. Eighty dollars? That's highway _____!
9. The _____ for the event was fantastic.
10. When did you finally _____ out the door for work?

DOWN

1. Sooner or _____ Todd plans to quit smoking.
2. Hurry up and get _____ for school.
3. Move over and make _____ for me.
4. Iris got a _____ at the doctor's office.
6. For the time _____ we shouldn't complain about it.
7. I'm staying home because I'm under the _____.

Unit 31
Describing People

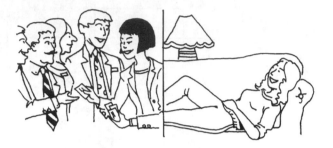

come across (as)   to be perceived as, to be judged as
also: **come off as**

USAGE NOTE: These idioms are used when talking about the impression that someone has on other people.

- Anthony discovered that he wasn't hired because he **came across** too strong during the job interview.
- Catherine may **come off as** a selfish person, but actually she can be very kind.

party pooper   someone who tries to reduce the interest or enthusiasm of others
USAGE NOTE: This idiom is used to describe someone who does not share the same interest as others and tries to discourage them.

- All of us want to go to Disneyland except Ellen. Why is she often such a **party pooper?**

penny-pincher   someone who is very careful about spending money
also: **tightwad, cheapskate**

- Mr. Steer is such a **penny-pincher** that he only buys used clothing at thrift stores.
- My dad is a real **tightwad**. He only gave me $10 to spend for my date with Julie!
- Miriam is a **cheapskate** for giving me a small box of candy on my birthday.

go-getter   enthusiastic worker or hard-working person
USAGE NOTE: This idiom is often preceded by the adjective *real*.

- I'm sure Alexandra will succeed in life because she's always been a **go-getter**.

show off   to let others see one's special possession or talent
related form: **show-off** (noun)

GRAMMAR/USAGE NOTES: The verbal form is separable when an object is used. The noun form usually expresses a negative meaning of disapproval.

- Faika **showed off** her new wedding dress to her friends.
- Brian thinks he has a wonderful voice, but to me he's just a big **show-off**.

know-it-all   someone who believes he or she knows more than others

- Don't try to convince Angela of your ideas. She's a **know-it-all**.
- No one listens to Greg at meetings because he always acts like such a **know-it-all**.

open-minded   willing to consider the values and opinions of others
   also: **broad-minded**
   opposite meaning: **narrow-minded** (unwilling to consider others' values and opinions)
   ■ A *narrow-minded* person may come across as a know-it-all to others who are more
      open-minded.
   ■ One of the challenges of today's world is for minority groups to learn how to be
      broad-minded about the cultural beliefs and values of other groups.

absent-minded   forgetful
   USAGE NOTE: This adjective form may be used with the noun *professor* to describe
   someone who fits the stereotype of a forgetful scholar.
   ■ Nate is always leaving the house without his wallet. Why is he so *absent-minded?*
   ■ My husband forgot our anniversary again! He's like an *absent-minded* professor.

easy-going   relaxed, unworried
   also: **laid-back**
   GRAMMAR NOTE: In some dictionaries, the main entry is one word.
   ■ It's a pleasure working for Mrs. Hansen because she's an *easy-going* boss.
   ■ Isaac is too *laid-back* to be a real go-getter in life.

EXERCISES

A.   **Fill in each blank with the missing part of the idiom.**

GAIL: What do you think of my friends you met last night?

NURIA: Well, in general they seem like easy-_____ people. I'm surprised
                                                        1
   how open-_____ most of them are.
                           2

GAIL: Very broad-minded. Did you notice how some of them like to show

   _____ their knowledge of current affairs?
              3

NURIA: Especially Dirk. He comes _____ as a _____-it-all.
                                                   4   5

GAIL: Yeah, but he's a nice guy. It's funny how _____-minded he can be.
                                                                6

NURIA: Yes, I noticed that he kept forgetting where his drink was. And what is it

   with Mindy? She kept checking the food on the table and cleaning up after

   everyone.

GAIL: Oh, Mindy, she's a real go-_____ about everything. And you should
                                            7
   see what a _____-pincher she is.
                        8

NURIA: In what way?

GAIL: She's always worried about how much things cost. Sometimes it gets so

   annoying when we go out that she's almost a party_____.
                                                                    9

NURIA: That's too bad. She should learn to be more laid-back about things!

B. Choose the statement in the right column that best responds to the question in the left column. Write the appropriate number in the blank.

 NOTE: *To do this as a listening exercise, cover up the left column before you start the tape.*

1. Do you see that man smiling and talking to Samantha?

_____ a. Maybe because you always come off as such a know-it-all!

2. Is Elizabeth always so narrow-minded about religion?

_____ b. Yes, he looks like a laid-back person.

3. I told you that the answer was 42. Why don't you ever listen to me?

_____ c. Well, he's never been much of a go-getter.

4. Isn't your husband too easy-going to succeed in life?

_____ d. Don't be such a tightwad!

5. Can you believe that this one cup of coffee costs two dollars?

_____ e. Yes, but she's much more open-minded about other things.

C. Use the idioms in your spoken or written answers to the following questions.

1. How does a college education help someone to become more **broad-minded?** Is this good or bad? Why?

2. Why do most people become **absent-minded** as they grow older? Is there any way to prevent this from happening?

3. Do you have a special skill or talent that you sometimes **show off?** What is it?

4. Do you know anyone who **comes across as** a **party pooper?** Describe how.

5. In what ways are you **easy-going** with money, and in what ways are you sometimes a **penny-pincher?**

D. Using the idioms from this unit, develop a dialogue or role play about your character or personality. You may include the following information:

▪ in what ways you consider yourself to be open-minded;

▪ in what ways you consider yourself to be narrow-minded;

▪ in what ways you can be a go-getter;

▪ in what ways you can be laid-back;

▪ whether you are ever absent-minded;

▪ whether you are ever a show-off.

Unit 32
Describing Things and Situations

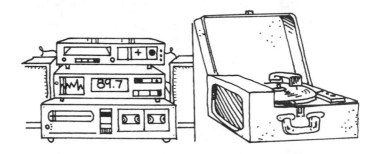

paint a picture   to describe a situation in a certain way

> USAGE NOTE: Adjectives such as *rosy* and *gloomy* are usually used.

- The nation's leading economist *painted a* rosy *picture* about continued growth in the automobile industry.
- The doctor *painted a* gloomy *picture* about my chances of walking again after the accident.

out of the ordinary   unusual, special

opposite meaning: **run of the mill** (average, ordinary)

> GRAMMAR NOTE: Hyphens (–) are needed when the expressions are used as adjectives before nouns.

- Axel came home after midnight last night. That's quite *out of the ordinary* for him.
- The police had to deal with several *out-of-the-ordinary* crimes this past week, including a kidnapping.
- I didn't really like the play because I thought the acting was *run of the mill.*

up to date   modern, current, timely

opposite meaning: **out of date** (old, not current)

> GRAMMAR NOTE: Hyphens are needed when these expressions precede nouns.

- The president of the United States constantly has to be kept *up to date* on international affairs.
- When we remodeled our house, we purchased *up-to-date* appliances and furnishings.
- This newspaper is a week *out of date*; can I recycle it?

first-rate   excellent, superior, of best quality

related idiom: **second-rate** (of average to poor quality)

> GRAMMAR NOTE: These expressions are usually used with hyphens.

- The meal and service were truly *first-rate*. Thanks for the wonderful evening.
- If you buy a *second-rate* stereo system, you won't get good sound quality.

out of this world   wonderful, fantastic, perfect

- The roast leg of lamb and potatoes in the oven smell *out of this world.*
- Our trip to Hawaii was *out of this world*. We can't wait to go back again.

spick and span   very clean, very neat
- Mary's kitchen looked *spick and span* before her in-laws came to visit.
- The sergeant examined the soldiers' uniforms to make sure they were *spick and span*.

brand new   in perfect, new condition

GRAMMAR NOTE: A hyphen is needed when the expression precedes a noun.
- Baron spent several thousand dollars on his 1945 Ford to make it look *brand new*.
- The Bigelows sold their old living room furniture and bought a *brand-new* set.

clear-cut   clearly stated, definite, obvious
also: **crystal clear**

GRAMMAR/USAGE NOTES: These idioms may be used with nouns such as *position* or *explanation*. Note that *clear-cut* normally occurs with a hyphen in all positions, while *crystal clear* usually doesn't.
- The manager took a *clear-cut* position on pay raises. There would be none this year.
- The professor's explanation of a molecule was *crystal clear* to everyone in the class.

be the pits   to be terrible, to be the worst

USAGE NOTE: This expression is used in informal conversations.
- This weather *is the pits*. We haven't seen the sun in weeks.
- It's *the pits* that I have two final exams in one day.

dog-earred   worn, well-used

USAGE NOTE: This idiom refers to books and other printed material.
- This paperback novel is quite *dog-earred.* You must have read it several times.
- The student reached for his *dog-earred* dictionary to find the definition.

EXERCISES

A.   **Fill in each blank with the missing part of the idiom.**

1. This is such a delicious meal. The main dish is truly out of this _____.

2. My neighbor asked me to watch his house to see that nothing out of the _____ happened.

3. The head of the Federal Reserve Board painted a grim _____ about the sudden rise in interest rates.

4. We bought more up-to-_____ equipment to modernize our office.

5. The kitchen of that gourmet restaurant is always kept _____ and span.

6. Our encyclopedia set has become so _____-earred and out of date that it's time to replace it.

7. This weather is the _____. It's been cloudy for weeks.

8. The doctor's advice to me was _____-cut: Quit smoking or face respiratory problems for the rest of my life.

9. That institute is first-_____ if you want to learn a foreign language such as German.

10. Andrea was very upset when she spilled oil on her _____-new dress.

B. Choose the statement in the right column that best responds to the question in the left column. Write the appropriate number in the blank.

NOTE: *To do this as a listening exercise, cover up the left column before you start the tape.*

1. Have you seen Sean's 1956 Chevy Bel Air convertible?

2. Don't you think that this is a suspenseful movie we're watching?

3. Was there anything out of the ordinary about the city council meeting?

4. Wouldn't you prefer to have a more up-to-date hairstyle?

5. Why are you painting such a gloomy picture about our financial situation?

____ a. I just want to be sure that the problem is crystal clear to you.

____ b. You're right. It's a first-rate thriller.

____ c. Not yet, but I heard that he made it look brand new.

____ d. No, we discussed the usual run-of-the-mill stuff.

____ e. Why? I don't think mine is out of date!

C. Use the idioms in your spoken or written answers to the following questions.

1. Have you ever had a day that *was the pits?* What happened?

2. Why do you think the unusual expression *dog-earred* is used to describe the pages of a well-used book?

3. What kind of job would be *out of the ordinary*, and what kind would be *run of the mill?*

4. Suggest some *clear-cut* values that all people of the world should respect.

5. Would you *paint a rosy* or *gloomy picture* about your own future? Why?

D. Using the idioms from this unit, develop a dialogue or role play about the condition of things in your house or apartment. You may include the following information:

- whether you generally keep your place spick and span;
- what items are brand new;
- whether your furnishings and appliances are up to date;
- what books or other materials are quite dog-earred;
- whether there's anything out of the ordinary about your place.

Unit 33
Ability and Experience

get the hang of   to learn how to do, to gain an understanding of
also: **get a feel for**

- I've tried skiing a couple of times, but I can't seem to *get the hang of* it.
- The police department allows citizens to *get a feel for* police work by riding along in patrol cars.

have a knack for   to have special talent or ability for

USAGE NOTE: The adjective *real* is often used.

- Irene should become an engineer because she *has a knack for* mathematics.
- Billy *has a* real *knack for* playing songs on the piano without having to read the music.

be right up one's alley   to be a suitable activity for someone

- The former professional soccer player agreed to coach the youth soccer team because it *was right up his alley.*
- Since you enjoy playing tennis, then racquetball should *be right up your alley* too.

be cut out for   to have the needed skill or ability for
also: **be cut out to be, have what it takes**

USAGE NOTE: These idioms are often used in the negative.

- As much as Chris wants to be a pro football player, he*'s* really not *cut out for* it.
- Dave's fear of flying means that he*'s* definitely not *cut out to be* a pilot.
- Brenda *has what it takes* to be a politician. She loves negotiating and debating.

know like the back of one's hand   to know very well, to have much experience
also: **have something down pat**

GRAMMAR/USAGE NOTES: Both idioms are separable. They are used when someone is very familiar with a certain route or procedure.

- Charlie *knows* the way home from work *like the back of his hand.*
- The new employee doesn't need more help operating the machine. She*'s got* it *down pat.*

102

lose one's touch   to fail at what one used to do well
- Recently I haven't been playing basketball very well. I must be *losing my touch.*
- Ms. Ochoa is *losing her touch* on the piano. She's never made so many mistakes before.

be all thumbs   to be very awkward or clumsy
also: **be born with two left feet**
- Karin *is all thumbs* when operating a computer. She's constantly pushing the wrong buttons.
- Pierre isn't very good at sports because he *was born with two left feet.*

wet behind the ears   inexperienced, immature
USAGE NOTE: This idiom is often used with the adverb *still.*
- Our baseball team didn't do very well this year because most of the players were still *wet behind the ears.*
- The new clerk is so *wet behind the ears* that he'll need a lot of on-the-job training.

have a green thumb   to be good at gardening
- The Wilson's garden is so green and beautiful. Mrs. Wilson really *has a green thumb.*
- I must not *have a green thumb* because every plant that I buy for my apartment dies!

EXERCISES

A.   Fill in each blank with the missing part of the idiom.

EARL: Mia, I'm not sure that I'm cut _____ for this managerial position.
                                         1

MIA: Why? Employee supervision is right up your _____ because you know
                                                          2
everyone's job like the back of your _____, don't you?
                                        3

EARL: Maybe, but recently I feel like I'm losing my _____.
                                                        4

MIA: What do you mean? Are you all _____ with the new computer
                                        5
equipment?

EARL: Exactly. I've had lots of training, but I still feel _____ behind the ears
                                                              6
when I show someone else how to operate it.

MIA: That's natural, Earl. I think your strength is that you have a real_____
                                                                            7
for relating to people well.

EARL: I'm not so sure now that I'm a manager. Sometimes I think I relate better to the
plants in my garden; at least I have a _____ thumb!
                                        8

MIA: Don't worry. You'll get the _____ of the new position eventually.
                                     9

B. Choose the statement in the right column that best responds to the question in the left column. Write the appropriate number in the blank.

 NOTE: *To do this as a listening exercise, cover up the left column before you start the tape.*

1. Can you help me repair my car? Something's wrong with the motor.

2. Stephanie has a real knack for numbers, doesn't she?

3. Have you ever seen anyone dance as badly as Mike?

4. Did you ever get the hang of rollerblading? I hear it's fun.

5. I thought you were good at billiards. Haven't you missed a lot of shots?

____ a. Not really. It seems like he was born with two left feet!

____ b. I've tried it a few times, but I haven't gotten a feel for it yet.

____ c. I'd be glad to. I know that engine like the back of my hand.

____ d. She sure does. Accounting would be right up her alley!

____ e. I certainly have. I must be losing my touch.

C. Use the idioms in your spoken or written answers to the following questions.

1. Is there any special skill that you ***have a knack for?***

2. Do you ***have*** English ***down pat*** yet, or are you still ***wet behind the ears?***

3. Do you know anyone who ***has a green thumb?*** What is that person like?

4. Would you ***have what it takes*** to be a politician? A soldier? Why or why not?

5. What happens to athletes when they ***lose their touch?***

D. Using the idioms from this unit, tell a classmate about your talents and abilities. You may include the following information:

- what job you think you're cut out for;
- whether you have a knack for sports;
- what hobbies are right up your alley;
- whether you've ever had a green thumb;
- whether you're losing your touch at anything.

Unit 34
Effort and Laziness

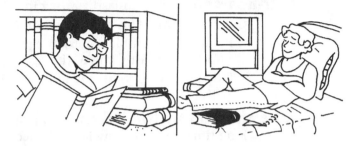

go all out   to make maximum effort
    also: **give it one's all**

- Our basketball team *went all out* to win the important championship game.
- No one will complain if you *give it your all* but still don't succeed.

burn the candle at both ends   to work hard day and night

- How can you go to school and keep two jobs? You must be *burning the candle at both ends!*

burn the midnight oil   to work hard through the night
    also: **pull an all-nighter**

- Jack had been postponing much of his schoolwork, so he had to *burn the midnight oil* before final exam week.
- If we want to finish this report by tomorrow, we'll have to *pull an all-nighter* here at the office.

keep up   to continue doing well

    GRAMMAR/USAGE NOTES: This idiom is separable. It is often followed by *the good work.*

- Fran is in third place at the halfway mark of the marathon. I wonder if she can *keep* it *up.*
- You're doing a wonderful job on this assignment. *Keep up* the good work.

get around to   to gradually accomplish or begin work on

    GRAMMAR/USAGE NOTES: This idiom is often followed by the pronoun *it* or a gerund (verb + *-ing*). It indicates that somebody is being lazy or slow to act.

- I'll paint the bedrooms when I can *get around to* it, OK? Don't keep bothering me about it.
- Harry has never *gotten around to* repaying the fifty dollars he owes me from last month.

drag one's feet   to be slow to move or act

    USAGE NOTE: This idiom indicates a lack of desire to do something.

- I told you a long time ago to get ready for bed. You're just *dragging your feet.*
- It's time Wilma stopped *dragging her feet* and told her boyfriend that their relationship has ended.

lift a finger   not to make any effort at all, not to bother to help

USAGE NOTE: This idiom is usually used in a negative sense when someone doesn't act to assist another person.

- Mrs. Waters is upset with her husband because he doesn't *lift a finger* to help with chores around the house on the weekend. He just watches sports programs on TV.
- When Christian's car had a flat tire in the parking lot, not a single person *lifted a finger* to help him.

half-hearted   unenthusiastic, rather uninterested

GRAMMAR NOTE: This adjective form is sometimes used as an adverb ending in *-ly.*

- Because of a terrible record of 2 wins and 13 losses, our team showed a *half-hearted* effort in the last game of the season.
- Billy often goes to his piano lessons *half-heartedly.* He'd rather be playing outside with his friends.

take the bull by the horns   to finally do something that one has delayed doing for a long time, to stop being lazy and accomplish something

- Lisa had postponed the assignment for so long that she finally had no choice but to *take the bull by the horns* and do it.
- It's already noon and half of Saturday is gone. I've got to *take the bull by the horns* and do some yardwork.

EXERCISES

A.   **Fill in each blank with the missing part of the idiom.**

1. The police report indicated that no one lifted a _____ to help the old lady when she was robbed.

2. If you _____ up the good work in college, it will benefit you greatly when you look for a job.

3. Our landlord said that he wasn't sure when he could get _____ to fixing the leaky faucet.

4. Ms. Fella has been burning the _____ oil trying to finish her book by the publisher's deadline.

5. The high school wrestling team went all _____ to qualify for statewide competition.

6. If you keep dragging your _____ like that, you'll never get it done.

7. A single mother with kids and a full-time job probably finds herself burning the _____ at both ends.

8. The garage was getting so crowded with junk that Diane finally took the bull by the _____ and cleaned it out.

9. When I asked my wife if she were willing to move to another state, her response was rather _____-hearted.

B. Choose the statement in the right column that best responds to the question in the left column. Write the appropriate number in the blank.

NOTE: *To do this as a listening exercise, cover up the left column before you start the tape.*

1. Have you made our plane reservations yet?

2. Was Timothy interested in going with us to Palm Springs?

3. Is anyone working with you now to finish the research report?

4. How did you get the research report done by today?

5. How did Mrs. Devine tell her husband that she wanted a divorce?

____ a. His response was rather half-hearted, if you ask me.

____ b. She just took the bull by the horns and told him clearly!

____ c. No, no one has lifted a finger to help me complete it.

____ d. Yes, I finally got around to contacting the ticket agent.

____ e. We stopped dragging our feet and pulled an all-nighter.

C. Use the idioms in your spoken or written answers to the following questions.

1. Why would someone be *half-hearted* about getting married? How do you feel about marriage?

2. When a crime is happening nearby, why might people not *lift a finger* to help? What would you do?

3. How do you *keep up* the good work in school or at a job?

4. What kind of job might require you to *burn the candle at both ends?* Would you want such a job? Why or why not?

5. What kinds of things do you *go all out* for?

D. Using the idioms from this unit, develop a presentation describing an important task that you made an effort to accomplish. You may include the following information:

- whether you dragged your feet about accomplishing the task or went all out from the beginning;
- whether there were times when you worked half-heartedly;
- whether you ever had to burn the midnight oil;
- whether anyone lifted a finger to help you;
- how you managed to keep up the good work.

Unit 35
Difficulty and Ease

run into trouble   to face difficulty, to encounter problems

also: **hit a snag**

USAGE NOTE: The adjectives *unexpected* or *unforeseen* can be used.

- The construction crew **ran into trouble** building the new highway because of the large rock formations just under the surface.
- The project would have been completed on time if the project team hadn't **hit an** unexpected **snag**.

be up against   to face as a difficulty or obstacle

GRAMMAR/USAGE NOTES: While having the same basic meaning as the previous entries, *be up against* requires an object that names the difficulty or obstacle.

- The president **is up against** stiff opposition on his new crime bill.
- Vera didn't know she was going to **be up against** the best runners in the state when she entered the marathon.

in a jam   in a difficult or embarrassing situation

also: **in a bind, in hot water**

USAGE NOTE: The adjective *real* is often added. *In hot water* is used when someone faces bad consequences for their actions.

- I'm **in a** real **jam**. My car won't start and I'm late for work. Could you give me a ride?
- Whenever Prenprapa is **in a bind**, she can always depend on her family and friends.
- You'll be **in hot water** if you leave work early without permission.

in dire straits   in a very difficult or terrible situation

also: **up a creek without a paddle, between a rock and a hard place**

- The desert hikers were **in dire straits** because they'd been lost for two days without water.
- We thought we were **up a creek without a paddle** when we left on vacation without our travelers' checks. However, we were able to replace them overnight.
- John's **between a rock and a hard place** at work because he hates his job but he can't afford to quit and find a new one.

be in over one's head   to be unprepared or unable to handle a situation
also: **bite off more than one can chew**

GRAMMAR NOTE: The main entry can be made plural. The term *way* can be added before *over* and *more*.

- As teenagers, Carl and Marie don't know how to care for their baby girl. I think they're in way **over their heads.**
- Harriet is trying her best to handle seven classes this semester, but I think she **bit off more than she can chew.**

open a can of worms   to cause problems that previously didn't exist, to change matters that were thought to be under control

USAGE NOTE: This idiom often involves the unfortunate mention of a sensitive topic.

- When my mother commented in front of everyone that my husband was gaining weight, she didn't realize that she had **opened a can of worms.**
- The National Congress **opened a can of worms** when it voted to give more power and fiscal responsibility to the individual states.

ups and downs   good and bad times, difficulties

GRAMMAR/USAGE NOTES: This idiom includes both good and bad periods of life, but is used mostly during the bad times. It is often preceded by a possessive pronoun.

- Jean and I have our **ups and downs**, but generally we have a good relationship.
- Artie has had many **ups and downs** during his long illness. Right now he's fine, though.

without a hitch   successfully, without difficulty

USAGE NOTE: This expression is often used with the idioms *to come off* or *to go off*, both meaning *to happen*.

- Despite limited practice sessions, opening night at the theater went off **without a hitch.**
- The veteran pilot has been flying airplanes for thirty years **without a hitch.**

be a piece of cake   to be very easy

USAGE NOTE: This idiom can also be used in an exclamation starting with *What . . . .*

- Don't worry about the quiz tomorrow. It'll **be a piece of cake** if you've studied at all.
- What **a piece of cake** it was to assemble this bicycle!

no-brainer   something that is simple and uncomplicated

- This homework is a **no-brainer**. I'll be done in five minutes.
- Irma loves to garden on the weekends because it's a **no-brainer** compared to her job.

EXERCISES

A.   **Fill in each blank with the missing part of the idiom.**

1. Even though the Andersons have some _____ and downs in their marriage, generally they're quite happy together.

2. The rescue of the injured rock climber went off without a _____.

3. The young politician felt that she was in over her _____ when she first arrived in Washington, D.C., but now she feels more comfortable.

4. The student council was up _____ strong resistance from the campus community for its plan to raise activity fees.

5. Because the central government has collapsed and the economy is poor, the small African nation finds itself in dire _____.

6. The supervisor opened a _____ of worms by suggesting that some workers were inefficient and might be fired.

7. We've hardly had any homework or major assignments in this class. What a _____ of cake it's been!

8. The housing project ran into _____ when a nest of rare birds was discovered on the property and all construction was stopped.

9. Rebecca was _____ a real jam because no baby-sitter was available to watch her children.

10. I didn't even have to study for the test. It was a real no-_____.

B. Choose the statement in the right column that best responds to the question in the left column. Write the appropriate number in the blank.

NOTE: *To do this as a listening exercise, cover up the left column before you start the tape.*

1. Why are you so late getting home?

2. Listen, I'm in a real jam. Could you lend me a hundred dollars?

3. Could you show me how to balance the checking account?

4. Did the board of directors accept your suggestion?

5. Did you hear that Donna was in hot water with the boss for her poor work?

____ a. No, I was up against opposition from two key members.

____ b. I ran into trouble at the garage. The car wasn't ready at 5:00 P.M.

____ c. No, but I knew she had bitten off more than she could chew.

____ d. Not this time. You always seem in dire straits with money.

____ e. I'd be glad to. It's really a no-brainer once you know how.

C. Use the idioms in your spoken or written answers to the following questions.

1. *Are* the exercises in this book *a piece of cake*, or do you sometimes *run into trouble?* How?

2. Suppose that you have important travel plans for the coming weekend. What can you do to make sure they go off *without a hitch?*

3. Have you ever *bitten off more than you could chew?* How did you resolve the situation?

4. What do the unusual expressions *up a creek without a paddle* and *between a rock and a hard place* literally mean, and why are they used to describe terrible situations that people have to face?

5. Topics like politics and religion are generally avoided in conversations because they often *open a can of worms.* How could this happen?

D. Using the idioms from this unit, develop a dialogue or role play about difficulties and problems in your life. You may include the following information:

- whether you've had ups and downs in a relationship with another person, in school, or at work;
- what you've been up against as a major obstacle in your life;
- whether you've ever been in dire straits, and what happened;
- whether you've ever opened a can of worms about a personal matter;
- what parts of your life you consider to be a piece of cake, and why.

Unit 36
Remembering and Forgetting

look back (on)   to remember part(s) of one's past life
- Old Mr. Jimenez loves to **look back on** the days when he was young and athletic.
- When I **look back on** what I did as a teenager, I'm amazed that I'm still alive today.

hold on to   to keep, to maintain
USAGE NOTE: This idiom is often used with the nouns *thought, feeling*, and *memory*.
- I like your suggestion that we buy all new furniture for our bedroom. **Hold on to** that thought for later.
- Even though Mr. Hanks's wife has been dead for several years, he still **holds on to** memories of their happy life together.

keep in mind   to make an effort to remember
also: **bear in mind**
- While you're shopping this afternoon, please **keep in mind** that we have to go to a meeting at five o'clock.
- Next time we invite Bernice for dinner, we should **bear in mind** that she doesn't like anything with tomatoes in it.

learn something by heart   to memorize
- The teacher expected the children to **learn** the new vocabulary **by heart.**
- The actress was having difficulty **learning** her new lines **by heart**, so she was replaced by another actress who had memorized the part completely.

on the tip of one's tongue   close to being remembered or said
USAGE NOTE: This idiom is used when someone has momentary difficulty remembering something, such as a name or number.
- Who was that lawyer we met last night? Her name is **on the tip of my tongue.**
- Jesse's telephone number is just **on the tip of my tongue.** I'll have it in just a moment.

pop into one's head   to suddenly remember or think of
- I couldn't remember the answer to the teacher's question, but then it suddenly **popped into my head.**
- The right numbers for the combination lock will **pop into your head** at any moment.

111

fade away   to disappear slowly as time passes

- At the time of the accident Ernie was very upset, but slowly his memory of the unpleasant incident has *faded away.*
- Even though we'll be separated for two months, don't let your love for me *fade away!*

slip one's mind   to be forgotten, not to be able to remember at the moment
also: **draw a blank**

GRAMMAR/USAGE NOTES: *Draw a blank* requires that the subject be the person who forgets, while *slip one's mind* requires that the possessive adjective *one's* refer to the person who forgets. The adverb *completely* can be used with *slip one's mind*, while the adjective *complete* is used with *draw a blank.*

- Ann was sorry that she didn't meet you for lunch today. It completely *slipped her mind.*
- What day is today? I'm *drawing a* complete *blank.*

not cry over spilt milk   not to continue to think about things that have already happened and can't be changed

- You can't change the fact that you lost your job, so *don't cry over spilt milk.*
- Karen still feels terrible about her divorce two years ago, but she fully realizes that she should*n't cry over spilt milk.*

forgive and forget   to finally decide to forget someone's past mistake

- You know that Manuel didn't mean to wreck your car last year. Isn't it time for you to *forgive and forget?*
- For years I've been upset at Mike for stealing my girlfriend and marrying her, but I now realize it's time to *forgive and forget.*

EXERCISES

A.   Fill in each blank with the missing part of the idiom.

1. The name of that new restaurant is on the _____ of my tongue. I'll remember it in a moment.

2. When you shop for my birthday present, keep in _____ that I don't need any more ties.

3. It's been a week since you lost your wallet, and it's not going to be found, so there's really no sense in crying over spilt _____.

4. Dorothy called the doctor to apologize for having let the appointment _____ her mind.

5. Becky is still angry at her former husband, but gradually she's learning to _____ and forget.

6. When I look _____ on my youth, I wonder how my parents were able to accept my bad attitude and behavior.

7. As soon as an idea for a new book _____ into my head, I write it down in a small notebook.

8. Antonio's memories of an unhappy childhood have slowly _____ away as the years have passed.

9. The Thompsons held _____ to the memory of their young daughter for many years after her death.

10. I try to learn the names of all my students by _____ during the first week of classes.

B. Choose the statement in the right column that best responds to the question in the left column. Write the appropriate number in the blank.

NOTE: *To do this as a listening exercise, cover up the left column before you start the tape.*

1. How can I ever speak to Lenora again after what she did to me?

2. Have you finished preparing your oral presentation yet?

3. Do you want to hear the idea that just popped into my head?

4. Can Pete and I ride our bikes to the bookstore quickly?

5. What's Coleen's new telephone number?

____ a. I'm drawing a blank, but wait—it's on the tip of my tongue.

____ b. Hold on to your thought, will you? I'm too busy to talk now.

____ c. Yes, but bear in mind that it will be dark soon.

____ d. Not quite yet. I've still got to learn it by heart.

____ e. I keep telling you—it's better to forgive and forget.

C. Use the idioms in your spoken or written answers to the following questions.

1. Do you ever *learn* the words to a song *by heart?* Is this easy or difficult for you to do?

2. Do the lyrics to any song *pop into your head* now?

3. What are some things that you have to *keep in mind* while you're driving?

4. Is there anyone whose actions you should *forgive and forget*, but for some reason can't?

5. When was the last time that someone was very unfair to you? In such a case, do you tend to *cry over spilt milk*, or are you more likely to let the memory *fade away?* Explain.

D. Using the idioms from this unit, tell a classmate about your memory. You may include the following information:

- the parts of your past life you most enjoy looking back on;
- the single most important memory you hold on to;
- what memories tend to fade away with time;
- the last important appointment or obligation that slipped your mind;
- whether you are good at keeping important dates and times in mind, or whether such details often slip your mind.

Unit 37
Finding and Locating

be after   to be trying to find, to pursue
also: **go after**
- The book that you'*re after* is no longer available at this library.
- The private investigator decided to *go after* the criminal, who had fled the country.

run across   to find something accidently or unexpectedly
also: **come across**
- While Tyson was cleaning out the garage, he *ran across* some old photos in a shoebox.
- The boys *came across* a twenty-dollar bill as they were running down the sidewalk.

come by   to obtain, to get
- How did you *come by* that old watch that you're wearing? It looks like an antique.
- The police *came by* the new evidence when they searched the victim's apartment.

look into   to investigate
also: **check into**
- The supervisor *looked into* the possibility that some workers were stealing tools from the jobsite.
- The government carefully *checks into* the background of every candidate for the Supreme Court.

find out   to learn or determine, to gain knowledge of
- When you see Ben, you need to *find out* the day and time of the next seminar.
- I'd like to *find out* why Angela is still angry at me.
- So Gene does know about the surprise birthday party. How did he *find out* about it?

come up with   to discover, to invent, to suggest
also: **think up**
- Alexander Graham Bell was the first to *come up with* a working model of the modern telephone.
- Leon always *comes up with* good suggestions for improving office procedures.
- Sandra *thought up* a good excuse for not going to the party with her parents.

look up   to find information about

GRAMMAR/USAGE NOTES: This idiom is separable and is generally used for information that is readily available in written form.

- Franco always has a dictionary ready to *look up* the meanings of new words.
- If you can't remember his telephone number, you can *look* it *up* in the directory.

read up on   to read about or research in detail

- Scientific knowledge is changing so quickly that scientists constantly have to *read up on* the latest developments in their fields.
- The Olsens *read up on* Japanese customs before their trip to Tokyo.

go over   to read, to review, to study

also: **look over, read over**

GRAMMAR NOTE: The alternate forms are separable when a pronoun is used.

- The teacher *went over* the answers to the questions on the test with the students.
- Please *look* this *over* carefully and correct any mistakes before mailing it.
- Did you take enough time to *read over* all your notes before the final exam?

turn up   to be found, to appear (after being lost or misplaced)

- Don't worry if you can't find your wallet. It'll *turn up* eventually.
- Fortunately, most children who run away from home *turn up* within several days.

EXERCISES

A.   **Fill in each blank with the missing part of the idiom.**

Felicia was worried about the term paper for her sociology class because she still hadn't _____ up with a good topic. She had gone _____
₁   ₂
her class notes and textbook many times, hoping to run _____ an
₃
interesting idea, but nothing had seemed right.

Then one day Felicia was in the library reading _____ on recent
₄
developments in sociology when she suddenly realized her purse was missing. She called the campus police, who came immediately to look _____ the
₅
situation. As the police checked around the library, they _____ out that
₆
a young boy had been seen walking around with no apparent purpose.

Soon the police noticed the boy sneaking out of the library and went _____ him. The boy succeeded in escaping, but not without dropping
₇
his high school identification card. The police called the school and asked a secretary to_____ up the boy's address. They were able to arrest him,
₈
but unfortunately Felicia's purse never _____ up.
₉

This experience gave Felicia the idea of writing her term paper on youth crime on college campuses. When the sociology teacher asked how she had _____ by such a topic, Felicia certainly had an interesting story to tell!
₁₀

115

B. Choose the statement in the right column that best responds to the question in the left column. Write the appropriate number in the blank.

NOTE: *To do this as a listening exercise, cover up the left column before you start the tape.*

1. How did you come up with that great idea for our vacation?

2. Have you come across the kitchen broom anywhere? I still can't find it.

3. Shouldn't we get a lawyer to look over the contract before we sign it?

4. How can I find out the address of this toy manufacturer?

5. Have you checked into the cost of renting a motor home?

_____ a. That's a good idea. I'll ask Mr. Inez to read it over for us.

_____ b. Not yet. I'll look into rental rates tomorrow if I have time.

_____ c. Oh, I've been reading up on Hawaii for a while now.

_____ d. Don't worry. It'll turn up eventually.

_____ e. You can look it up in the reference section of the library.

C. Use the idioms in your spoken or written answers to the following questions.

1. What kind of excuses do students *think up* when they're late for class?

2. What would you do if you *came across* a large bag of money, and nobody saw you?

3. What person or place in the world are you most interested in *reading up on?*

4. What is your most valuable possession? How did you *come by* it?

5. What is the last thing you lost or misplaced that still hasn't *turned up?*

D. Using the idioms from this unit, develop a presentation describing some research you have done. You may include the following information:

- what general information you were after;
- whether you'd read up on it for class or for work;
- what material you had to go over in order to get the research information;
- whether anyone else was looking into the subject with you;
- how long it took for you to look the information up.

Unit 38
Understanding

get it   to understand

USAGE NOTE: This idiom is often used when someone requires time to understand.

- After Faye explained the procedure to Stanley a couple of times, he finally **got it**.
- Oh, so that's what you're trying to say. I **get it!**

catch on   to understand, to be a quick learner

- Once Ted is taught something, he usually remembers. He **catches on** very quickly.
- Most children who try to learn a second language can **catch on** easily.

figure out   to find an answer to, to solve, to understand
also: **make sense (of)**

GRAMMAR/USAGE NOTES: *Figure out* is separable, and can also be used for trying to understand a person's character.

- Jean's father helped her to **figure out** the difficult math problem.
- I can't **make sense of** this note from Ed. What is he trying to say?
- Sometimes Scott is very nice, and other times he's very selfish. I can't **figure** him **out**.

see someone's point   to understand someone's opinion or thought
also: **catch one's drift**

- I interrupted Craig's long explanation by saying, "OK, I **see your point.**"
- Jeff isn't the best student, if you **catch my drift.**

get the message   to finally understand the consequences of a situation or action
also: **see the writing on the wall**

- The school counselor told Sarah that she'd better **get the message** about the importance of school or she'd regret it for the rest of her life.
- Sahli finally **saw the writing on the wall** when the judge threatened to send him to jail on his next offense. He hasn't been in trouble with the law since then.

not make head or tail of   not to be able to understand at all

GRAMMAR/USAGE NOTES: This idiom is always used with *can* or *could*. The nouns *head* and *tail* are often made plural.

- We could**n't make head or tail of** Aunt Emma's handwriting in her letter to us.
- **Can** you **make heads or tails of** the last section of our physics book? I can't.

be beyond   not to be understood by someone
also: **go right over someone's head**

UsAGE NOTE: The subject of these expressions is the idea or situation that cannot be understood by someone.

- The fact that Bruce never eats any kind of meat *is beyond* me.
- Most of Lena's friends laughed at her joke, but it *went right over Drew's head.*

be Greek to   not to be understood by someone

GRAMMAR/USAGE NOTES: This expression is similar to the preceding entry, except that the reason for not understanding is usually the technical or obscure nature of the topic. The adjective *all* and the verb *sound* can also be used.

- Thanks for trying to explain the topic for your doctoral thesis, but it'*s* all *Greek to* me.
- I tried to explain Einstein's theory of relativity to my friend, but it just *sounded Greek to* him.

go in one ear and out the other   not to be understood (due to lack of interest)

- Betty tries to teach her children the right values, but often her words seem to *go in one ear and out the other.*
- Jack just sits in class daydreaming most of the time. Everything just *goes in one ear and out the other.*

get wrong   to misunderstand
related idiom: **get backwards** (to understand the opposite)

GRAMMAR/USAGE NOTES: These expressions must be separated. The object is the person or thing that is misunderstood.

- Don't *get* me *wrong*. I think your suggestion is a good one, but I wonder if it'll really work for this situation.
- No, Francis is the one who wants to stay home. I want to go. You *got* it *backwards.*

EXERCISES

A. Fill in each blank with the missing part of the idiom.

1. Do you think that Lydia will ever get the _____ about Sam and divorce him?

2. You got the meeting time _____—it's 7:00 P.M., not 6:00 P.M.

3. No matter how many times I explained how I felt, he never saw my _____.

4. Mr. Jenkins consulted a lawyer because he couldn't make __ _____ or tails of the fine print in the lease agreement.

5. Just watch how I move my feet on the dance floor and you'll _____ on.

6. Don't try explaining it to Monica. It'll just go in one _____ and out the other.

7. Josh is usually reasonable, but sometimes it's hard to _____ him out.

8. It's _____ me why Judy chooses to live alone with a houseful of cats.

9. Vera repeated her joke for me, and only then did I finally _____ it.

10. These mathematical symbols and equations are all _____ to me.

B.   Choose the statement in the right column that best responds to the question in the left column. Write the appropriate number in the blank.

NOTE: *To do this as a listening exercise, cover up the left column before you start the tape.*

1. Can you figure out what's wrong with my car?

2. Did you understand any part of yesterday's lecture?

3. How did Mr. Thomas finally get the message about drinking while driving?

4. Are you saying that you got the dates backwards and that now you can go?

5. Would you be interested in visiting the art museum?

____ a. Actually, the whole talk went right over my head.

____ b. Sorry, engines are all Greek to me.

____ c. Thirty days in jail helped him see the writing on the wall.

____ d. The idea really doesn't excite me, if you catch my drift.

____ e. You got it!

C.   Use the idioms in your spoken or written answers to the following questions.

1. When you listen to English, do you *catch on* quickly or slowly? Why?

2. What do you do if someone's joke *goes right over your head?*

3. Do you think that most young people pay attention to what their parents say, or does parental advice usually *go in one ear and out the other?* What is your case?

4. Have you ever been in some kind of serious trouble and then *seen the writing on the wall?* If possible, can you explain what happened?

5. Can you *make heads or tails* of today's world? What are our greatest problems and how can we solve them? Share your thoughts.

D.   Using the idioms from this unit, develop a dialogue about times when you had problems in understanding. You may include the following information:

- a time when something was Greek to you;
- a time when you got something backwards;
- a time when something your parents told you went in one ear and out the other;
- a time when you couldn't figure something out;
- a time when you caught on quickly.

Unit 39
Informing and Reporting

fill in (on)   to inform
also: **bring up-to-date**

GRAMMAR NOTE: These idioms must be separated so that the object follows the verb.

- The president depends on his advisors to *fill* him *in on* new developments each day.
- Mrs. Ramon's assistant *brought* her *up-to-date* when she returned from vacation.

keep posted   to keep informed

GRAMMAR NOTE: An object follows the verb, except in passive form.

- Would you please *keep* me *posted* on any progress in the baseball strike?
- The mayor of the city asked to be *kept posted* during the earthquake disaster.

spread the word   to distribute or send information
also: **put the word out**

- TV commercials are effective ways to *spread the word* about a new product.
- The supervisor *put the word out* that the new position of team leader was available to qualified applicants.

catch up on   to become informed about the current affairs of others

USAGE NOTE: This idiom is used when exchanging information about family and friends.

- Every year our family gathers at Thanksgiving and *catches up on* what's been happening.

keep up on   to maintain knowledge of, to have information on
also: **keep up with**

- I read the newspaper every day to *keep up on* current affairs.
- It's difficult to *keep up with* all the technological changes that are occurring.

What's the scoop?   What's the latest information?, What's happening?

- Someone told me that Sandy was hospitalized yesterday. *What's the scoop?*
- I heard that Antoine quit his job. *What's the scoop?*

fill out   to provide (in writing) the required information
> also: **fill in**
>
> GRAMMAR/USAGE NOTES: These idioms are separable. *Fill out* refers to an entire form, while *fill in* refers to the individual blanks on a form.
>
> ■ Please *fill out* the application form and then stand in that line.
>
> ■ You forgot to *fill* one of the blanks *in* with your Social Security number.

first-hand   directly from the original information source
> also: **straight from the horse's mouth**
>
> related idiom: **second-hand** (not from the original information source)
>
> ■ The newspaper reporter made sure that she got *first-hand* information for her article.
>
> ■ How do I know that Patti left her husband? I heard it *straight from the horse's mouth!*
>
> ■ The police couldn't arrest the suspect because most of the evidence was *second-hand.*

break the news   to reveal new information
> ■ The company president *broke the news* to shareholders that profits were down 25 percent.
>
> ■ I hate to *break the news* to you, but it's supposed to rain all weekend.

hot off the press   just published or released to the public
> ■ News of another major oil spill in the North Sea was *hot off the press.*
>
> ■ This headline is *hot off the press*—"Radical Terrorists Bomb Frankfurt Airport."

EXERCISES

A.   **Fill in each blank with the missing part of the idiom.**

1. You forgot to _____ out the back of the application form.

2. Sam is certain that his information is correct because he got it _____-hand.

3. The local community newspaper was the first one to _____ the news of the political scandal.

4. Emile keeps _____ on developments in his field by reading the trade journals.

5. The school office _____ the word of a new outbreak of measles.

6. The president's advisors kept him _____ on the international crisis.

7. I'm glad we could meet for coffee and _____ up on what's happening.

8. Is it true that Mark was fired from work? What's the _____?

9. News of fresh evidence in the murder trial was _____ off the press.

10. The marketing director filled the company president _____ on the new advertising campaign.

B. Choose the statement in the right column that best responds to the question in the left column. Write the appropriate number in the blank.

 NOTE: *To do this as a listening exercise, cover up the left column before you start the tape.*

1. Did I fill out this application form correctly?

2. Who brought you up-to-date on the new marketing campaign?

3. Which newspaper was first to have an article about the president's illness?

4. Have you been keeping up on the baseball championship?

5. Didn't you hear second-hand about Mr. Baker's tax problem?

____ a. No, I learned about it straight from the horse's mouth!

____ b. No, you forgot to fill in your Social Security number.

____ c. Ms. Smith filled me in this morning.

____ d. No, I haven't. What's the scoop?

____ e. I believe the *Los Angeles Mirror* broke the news.

C. Use the idioms in your spoken or written answers to the following questions.

1. How do you *keep posted* about news of your family?

2. What are some times of the year when families get together and *catch up on* old times? When did your family do this last?

3. Try to think of a serious problem that would require the police to *spread the word* to the community. How would they *put the word out?*

4. When a major problem develops, why do newspapers compete to be the first to *break the news?* What kind of problems can this cause?

5. What news stories are *hot off the press* this week?

D. Using the idioms from this unit, develop a presentation about a newspaper reporter's job. You may include the following information:

- how the reporter is able to keep up on community affairs;
- who first fills the reporter in on a new scandal or controversy in the community;
- whether that person learned about it first-hand or second-hand;
- why it's important to the reporter to be the first to break the news;
- how the reporter will keep posted on future developments.

Unit 40
Discussing and Interrupting

bring up   to mention, to introduce a topic
also: **come up**

GRAMMAR/USAGE NOTES: *Bring up* is separable, and the subject is the person who mentions an idea. The subject of *come up* is the idea itself.

- At the staff meeting one teacher **brought up** the question of safety on the playground.
- The school principal promised to **bring** the matter **up** before the school board.
- Many concerned teachers were glad that the issue had finally **come up.**

speak up   to express one's opinion

- Many citizens **spoke up** at the town council meeting to complain about tax increases.
- If you really have something to add to the discussion, don't hesitate to **speak up.**

raise a question   to inquire, to ask a question

GRAMMAR NOTE: *The* and *another* can be substituted for *a.*

- I wanted to **raise a question** during the public hearing but I didn't get a chance.
- Nearby residents **raised the question** of noise pollution from the proposed amusement park planned for their community.

go into   to discuss in detail, to cover thoroughly

- The special two-hour news program **went into** all sides of the environmental issue.
- Marvin and Krista spent weeks **going into** their problems with a marriage counselor.

touch on   to discuss briefly or superficially

- The president's State of the Union address **touched on** many issues and problems facing the country.
- The teacher **touched on** the major points that would be tested on the final exam.

kick around   to discuss casually

GRAMMAR/USAGE NOTES: The idiom is separable. It is used to discuss matters for which there is no urgent need for a decision.

- We don't have to make a quick decision on that matter. Let's spend some time **kicking** it **around.**
- The other staff members **kicked around** my suggestion that we have an office party.

123

cover ground   to cover much information, to discuss many details

USAGE NOTE: Expressions such as *too much* and *a lot of* can be added.

- The orientation session was good, but it **covered** too much **ground** in a short period of time.
- The teacher **covered** a lot of **ground** in her last lecture, so the test will be given a day earlier.

go off on a tangent   to discuss something not directly related to the main topic

- We didn't cover much ground in this seminar because the leader often **went off on a tangent.**
- Fabio tends to **go off on a tangent** in conversations and to bore everyone with his personal philosophy.

break in   to interrupt

also: **cut in**

related idiom: **cut off** (to refuse to allow someone to continue)

USAGE NOTE: *Cut off* is separable.

- During my speech someone **broke in** rudely and asked a stupid question, which I ignored.
- Sue was talking on the phone when her mother **cut in** to make an important call.
- When a board member tried to argue the issue further, the chairperson **cut** him **off.**

get a word in edgewise   to force one's way into a discussion

USAGE NOTE: This idiom is used when people try to express themselves while others are busy talking or arguing. It is often used in the negative.

- Murphy's friends were lost in a heated discussion, and Murphy couldn't **get a word in edgewise.**
- Everyone at the meeting was talking at the same time, but I finally managed to **get a word in edgewise.**

EXERCISES

A.   **Fill in each blank with the missing part of the idiom.**

1. The TV documentary covered too much _____ in its treatment of the Civil War.

2. Excuse me, but we're going off on a _____. Could we return to the main topic?

3. Before we begin today, let me briefly _____ on the main points from last week's lecture.

4. Lynn loves to talk and talk, so it's hard to get a _____ in edgewise.

5. The manager left the room before Brent had a chance to _____ another question.

6. If you think it's an important issue, why didn't you _____ it up earlier?

7. Sometime I'd like to sit down with you and _____ into this matter more carefully.

8. The Nelsons kicked _____ the idea of moving, but they finally decided against it.

9. I'm sorry to _____ in, but there's an important phone call for you.

10. Why do you stay so quiet during meetings? You should _____ up more!

B. Choose the statement in the right column that best responds to the question in the left column. Write the appropriate number in the blank.

NOTE: *To do this as a listening exercise, cover up the left column before you start the tape.*

1. Were you able to go into your marriage problems with your new counselor?

2. Did the training session cover a lot of ground?

3. Do you mind if I break in and raise a question?

4. Did Steve bring up any of the points he wanted to make?

5. Did you and your friends decide where to have the picnic?

____ a. Not really. The leader kept going off on a tangent.

____ b. No, on the first visit we were only able to touch on them.

____ c. Actually, he wasn't able to get a word in edgewise.

____ d. Please speak up whenever you have something to ask.

____ e. We kicked around several ideas and finally chose the beach.

C. Use the idioms in your spoken or written answers to the following questions.

1. When you are learning a new language, why is it important to *speak up* at every opportunity? Do you try to do this?

2. Do you feel comfortable *cutting in* when a group of people are discussing something? Why or why not?

3. When might it be necessary to *cut* someone *off?*

4. Most TV news programs just *touch on* major events instead of *going into* them. Why is this true? Can you see any possible problem with this?

5. In any kind of discussion, some people tend to *go off on a tangent.* Why does this happen? How can it be avoided?

D. Using the idioms from this unit, develop a dialogue or role play about a group discussion you are involved in. You may include the following information:

- who brings up the topic of discussion;
- what kinds of questions are raised;
- whether someone breaks in while you are talking;
- whether anyone ever goes off on a tangent;
- whether anyone has trouble getting a word in edgewise;
- how long you kick the topic around.

Review: Units 31–40

A. Circle the expression that best completes each sentence.

1. Mrs. Olson likes to _____ the days that she spent on a farm in the country.
   a. slip her mind
   b. look back on
   c. fill in

2. After days of kicking ideas around, suddenly a good solution to the problem _____.
   a. caught on
   b. went off on a tangent
   c. popped into my head

3. We enjoyed our meal at the _____ restaurant you spread the word about.
   a. first-rate
   b. show-off
   c. first-hand

4. It's natural for even the best of marriages to have some _____.
   a. run of the mill
   b. ups and downs
   c. party pooper

5. Arlene wasn't sure she was _____ police work, but she decided to apply anyway.
   a. caught up on
   b. held on to
   c. cut out for

6. I was lucky when I quickly _____ the information I needed for my term paper.
   a. ran across
   b. went into
   c. was after

7. At first Craig was dragging his feet on the project, but finally he _____ and completed it.
   a. knew it like the back of his hand
   b. took the bull by the horns
   c. painted a picture

8. I'll remember her name any moment now. It's _____.
   a. on the tip of my tongue
   b. learned by heart
   c. in over my head

9. It's easier to _____ if you keep an open-minded attitude about other people.
   a. break the news
   b. hit a snag
   c. forgive and forget

10. Have you _____ a good name for your baby yet?
    a. kept up
    b. gotten the hang of
    c. come up with

B. Indicate whether each statement is TRUE (T) or FALSE (F).

_____ 1. If something is clear-cut, then you can figure it out.
_____ 2. An easy-going person would probably not burn the candle at both ends.
_____ 3. If you get the message, then it goes in one ear and out the other.
_____ 4. Something would probably slip the mind of an absent-minded person.
_____ 5. If you have something down pat, then you're in over your head.
_____ 6. A narrow-minded person runs into trouble seeing another person's point.
_____ 7. Playing the piano would be right up your alley if you're all thumbs.
_____ 8. If you've been dragging your feet in your studies, then you'll have to give it your all to pass the course.
_____ 9. Sometimes you have to break in if you want to get a word in edgewise.
_____ 10. A penny-pincher would often eat out at first-rate restaurants.

C. Complete the puzzle with the missing parts of the idioms from the sentences below.

ACROSS

1. Your garden shows that you have a green _____.
6. The food at this restaurant is out of this _____.
7. Did anyone raise the _____ of cost?
8. The rescue of the injured hiker was made without a _____.
10. No one lifted a _____ to help us.
11. What's out of the _____ for one person is run of the mill for another.
12. Could you make head or _____ of his message?

DOWN

2. I heard the news straight from the horse's _____.
3. I didn't study enough, so I had to pull an all- _____ before the test.
4. Where can I _____ out her address?
5. His name is on the tip of my _____.
9. The workers burned the _____ oil repairing the broken pipe.

Unit 41
Happiness and Sadness

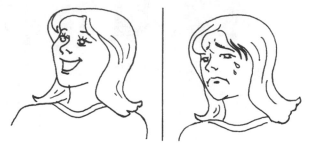

be all smiles　to be very happy
- Jessica *was all smiles* when she learned that she'd won the talent contest.
- Why *is* Igor *all smiles?* Did he just win the lottery or something?

be in seventh heaven　to be extremely happy
also: **be floating on cloud nine, be (sitting) on top of the world**
USAGE NOTE: These idioms convey the idea of an almost magical happiness.
- May and Ed have been married only two months, and they'*re* still *in seventh heaven* together.
- Becky *was floating on cloud nine* after she got the job.
- Jason just won the lottery, and now he'*s sitting on top of the world.*

grin from ear to ear　to smile broadly
GRAMMAR NOTE: This expression is often used in a continuous verb form.
- My son Hank was *grinning from ear to ear* when we gave him permission to go to Florida for spring break.

make one's day　to make someone very happy
USAGE NOTE: This idiom is usually used with the possessive adjective *my*.
- It really *made my day* when the boss commented on what a great job I was doing.
- When Carl got me a gift and card for my birthday, he really *made my day.*

happy camper　someone who is happy or satisfied with a situation
USAGE NOTE: This expression is often used in the negative to express dissatisfaction with a situation.
- Frieda was not a *happy camper* when she was assigned new responsibilities in the newsroom.
- The baseball player told management that he was not a *happy camper* and wanted to be traded to another team.

be down　to be unhappy
also: **feel down**
related idiom: **bring down** (to make someone feel unhappy)
- Linda *was down* because she hadn't done well on the real estate licensing exam.
- It's not unusual to *feel down* on rainy days.
- News of my brother's accident *brought* the whole family *down.*

128

feel blue   to feel sad, to feel depressed
     also: **be down in the dumps**
- Whenever my parents fly back home after visiting me, I **feel blue** for a while.
- Why **is** Marcio **down in the dumps** today? Did he get some bad news again?

have (on) a long face   not to smile, to show one's unhappiness
     USAGE NOTE: When *on* is not used, the adverb *such* is usually added.
- Little Mikey **had on a long face** when he was told he couldn't go outside to play.
- Why do you **have such a long face?** It's too nice a day to feel sad.

be a tear-jerker   to be a source of sadness, to show a very sad situation
     GRAMMAR/USAGE NOTES: In some dictionaries, *tear-jerker* is spelled as one word. The word *real* is often added before it.
- I didn't enjoy that movie very much because it **was a** real **tear-jerker.**
- The picture of a poor little girl begging for food on the streets **was a** real **tear-jerker,** so we readily agreed to donate some money to the relief organization.

lift one's spirits   to make someone feel better
- My fiftieth birthday made me feel old, so my friends **lifted my spirits** by taking me out for dinner.
- News that the infection had stopped spreading **lifted the patient's spirits.**

EXERCISES

A.   **Fill in each blank with the missing part of the idiom.**

1. News of the promotion I'd been waiting for really made my _____.
2. Noah was grinning from _____ to ear when he learned that his book had been accepted for publication.
3. Randall and Karen are in Paris on their honeymoon. They must be in seventh _____ right now.
4. Nicky had on a _____ face because she had to go to the dentist's office.
5. Many people in the audience were crying because the movie was a real _____-jerker.
6. Louis is actively looking for another job because he's not a happy _____ at work right now.
7. Sara and Jeff were all _____ as they announced their engagement.
8. Mr. McTaggart feels _____ because he continues to have many health problems.
9. A visit from his son's family lifted Mr. McTaggart's _____.
10. Inez has been _____ for days due to a death in her family.

B. Choose the statement in the right column that best responds to the question in the left column. Write the appropriate number in the blank.

NOTE: *To do this as a listening exercise, cover up the left column before you start the tape.*

1. Wasn't that novel a real tear-jerker?

_____ a. I remembered that animals always lift your spirits.

2. Why does Larry have on a long face?

_____ b. Yes, these days I'm not at all a happy camper.

3. How did you know getting a dog at the pet shop would make my day?

_____ c. Yes, it made me feel blue too.

4. Why are the Madisons all smiles?

_____ d. Oh, he's down in the dumps about problems at school.

5. Did something happen again at work to bring you down?

_____ e. They're floating on cloud nine about winning the lottery.

C. Use the idioms in your spoken or written answers to the following questions.

1. Does bad weather ever make you *feel blue?* Why does this happen?
2. Do you like to see movies or to read books that *are* real *tear-jerkers?* Why or why not?
3. What kind of news would make you *grin from ear to ear?*
4. Why *are* newlyweds usually *floating on cloud nine?* Does this feeling last? Why?
5. What are some reasons why someone might not to be a *happy camper* at work or at school?

D. Using the idioms from this unit, develop a dialogue or role play about an event or situation that brought you sadness in the beginning but later brought you happiness. You may include the following information:

- what first made you feel down;
- how long you felt blue;
- whether you showed your feelings by having on a long face;
- what eventually lifted your spirits or made your day;
- how finally you were all smiles;
- whether you're still a happy camper.

Unit 42
Anger and Annoyance

see red   to become very angry
also: **turn red, turn purple**
- Ned *sees red* every time someone makes a joke about his handicapped sister.
- I *turned red* with anger when Jane accused me of lying about the club's financial situation.
- Nicole is so upset she's *turning purple.*

tick off   to cause someone to be both angry and annoyed at the same time
- What *ticks* me *off* is that the government is wasting most of our tax dollars.
- Ethan was *ticked off* at his girlfriend for having forgotten his birthday.

raise one's voice   to express oneself in a loud, angry voice
- The teacher had to *raise her voice* to get the students to pay attention.
- Don't *raise your voice* at me, son. Just do what I tell you.

have a short fuse   to be easily angered
opposite meaning: **have a long fuse**
- Alan would be a good administrator if he didn't *have a short fuse* whenever someone challenged his decision-making.
- Mr. Peters has learned to control his emotions, so now he *has a long fuse.*

hit the roof   to suddenly become very angry
also: **hit the ceiling**
- Mrs. Wallace *hit the roof* when she saw her son's terrible school grades.
- I couldn't believe how my boss *hit the ceiling* when I told him about the serious computer error.

lose one's temper   to become so angry as to lose self-control
also: **blow one's stack**
USAGE NOTE: *Blow one's stack* is more informal than *lose one's temper.*
- Gina never *loses her temper* in public. She always manages to stay calm no matter what happens.
- The basketball coach *blew his stack* and yelled at his players for losing the important game.

storm off (to)   to leave suddenly in anger
  also: **storm out (of)**
  ■ When Hazel's parents refused to let her go on a date that night, she just *stormed off to* her bedroom.
  ■ Mrs. Fares *stormed out of* the house in the middle of an argument with her husband.

be a pain in the neck   to be annoying in an unpleasant way
  ■ My in-laws *are* such *a pain in the neck* when they come to visit once a year.
  ■ Donald hates to do homework. For him it's just *a pain in the neck.*

drive one crazy   to annoy greatly
  also: **drive up the wall**
  ■ It *drives me crazy* to hear the sound of a knife scraping on a plate.
  ■ Andrew's constant whistling really *drives me up the wall*. I wish he'd stop it.

blow off steam   to release one's anger or annoyance in a constructive way
  ■ Whenever Leandra gets angry, she *blows off steam* by running for several miles.
  ■ Working out at the gym is my favorite way of *blowing off steam.*

EXERCISES

A.   **Fill in each blank with the missing part of the idiom.**

1. There's no reason to raise your _____ when talking calmly would be more effective.

2. Mr. Folsom was so angry that he had to go outside and work in the garden to blow off _____ .

3. It drives me _____ when someone shakes their leg nervously against a table or chair.

4. The tremendous amount of homework in this class is a _____ in the neck.

5. Mrs. Bonnett can get angry so easily. She really has a _____ fuse.

6. Gail _____ off to the lounge when her boss unfairly criticized the quality of her work in front of others.

7. I can't remember the last time that I saw my Dad _____ his stack like this.

8. The patient's wife _____ the roof when she was told that the doctors had mistakenly removed her husband's good leg instead of his bad one.

9. The teacher saw _____ when she discovered that several students had cheated on the exam.

10. If you hadn't tried to lie to me, I wouldn't be so ticked _____ .

B. Choose the statement in the right column that best responds to the question in the left column. Write the appropriate number in the blank.

NOTE: *To do this as a listening exercise, cover up the left column before you start the tape.*

1. Look at Melissa. Isn't she turning red with anger?	____ a. I'm shouting at you because you really ticked me off.
2. Aren't small children a pain in the neck sometimes?	____ b. I was just trying to blow off some steam after our argument.
3. Why did Jordan lose his temper about such a simple problem?	____ c. I'd say she's turning purple.
4. Why are you raising your voice at me like that?	____ d. Yes, they often drive me up the wall.
5. Why did you storm out of the house and start lifting weights in the garage?	____ e. I guess because he has a really short fuse.

C. Use the idioms in your spoken or written answers to the following questions.

1. Is it ever necessary for parents to *raise their voices* at children? Why or why not?
2. What are some common things in life that can *be a pain in the neck?*
3. Do you *have a short fuse* or *a long fuse?* Explain.
4. Give an example of a situation or event that would cause someone to *hit the ceiling.*
5. What do people do to *blow off steam* when they're upset?

D. Using the idioms from this unit, tell a classmate about how someone angered you, how you responded, and how the situation ended. You may include the following information:

- what happened that ticked you off;
- whether you just raised your voice or whether you blew your stack;
- whether you stormed off in anger;
- whether you did anything to blow off steam;
- whether the situation is resolved or whether it's still driving you crazy.

133

Unit 43
Waiting, Patience, and Delay

hold on   to wait, to be patient
also: **hang on**

USAGE NOTE: *Hold on* is used in Unit 12 for waiting on the telephone. Here it is used in its more general meaning. Time expressions such as *just a second*, *just a minute*, and *just a moment* can be used with these idioms.

- Nuri asked Mohamed to *hold on* while she finished getting dressed.
- Could you *hang on* just a second? I'm expecting a phone call shortly.

be with   to give attention to someone after a period of waiting

USAGE NOTE: This expression is often followed by *shortly* or *in a moment*.

- Ted thought he'd have to wait a long time, but the salesperson *was with* him shortly.
- Please take a seat over there. I'll *be with* you in a moment.

kill time   to pass time doing nothing special

GRAMMAR/USAGE NOTES: The preposition *by* and a gerund (verb + *-ing*) usually follow this idiom.

- While Ian was waiting in the doctor's office, he *killed time* by reading a magazine.
- During the long drive to San Francisco, we *killed time* by playing word games.

tie up   to occupy, to keep busy

GRAMMAR/USAGE NOTES: *Tie up* is separable but is commonly used in the passive form. The idiom is often used when someone is so busy that they are unavailable for other purposes.

- Walter couldn't get much work done because a number of visitors *tied* him *up*.
- I'm sorry I can't help you to move because I'*m* all *tied up* this weekend.

put off   to postpone
also: **put on the back burner**
related idiom: **call off** (to cancel)

GRAMMAR/USAGE NOTES: These expressions are separable. *Put off* and *put on the back burner* are used when an activity will happen later; *call off* is used when the activity will never happen again.

- The cold, cloudy weather forced us to *put* the beach party *off* for a week.
- It wasn't the right time to introduce the new policy, so we *put* it *on the back burner*.
- Why did the boss *call off* the party after all the arrangements had been made?

134

sit on   to postpone by failing to act

> USAGE NOTE: This idiom is used when persons of authority choose not to take action.

- Although the boss had promised to make a decision about pay raises, he just *sat on* the matter for months.
- The bill never became law because the congressional committee *sat on* it too long.

hold up   to delay

> GRAMMAR/USAGE NOTES: This idiom is separable, and the object is usually the person or thing that is delayed.

- Unusually heavy air traffic *held* our plane *up* from landing for over an hour.
- I'm sorry I'm late. I was *held up* by a small household emergency.

run late   to be delayed, often because of one's own poor planning

> GRAMMAR NOTE: This idiom is usually used in a continuous verb form.

- Don't bother to make any breakfast for me. I'm *running* quite *late.*
- Charles didn't have time to go to the gym because he was *running late* at work.

wait out   to be patient by not acting too quickly
also: **stick out**

> GRAMMAR NOTE: These idioms are separable.

- Instead of going into the building after the heavily armed criminal, the police decided to encircle it and *wait* him *out.*
- Cindy thought she'd have to drop the difficult computer class, but she *stuck* it *out* and eventually was able to pass.

EXERCISES

A.   Fill in each blank with the missing part of the idiom.

1. Mark was running _____ for work because he had forgotten to set the alarm.

2. Thanks for coming. I'll be _____ you in a minute.

3. Could you _____ on for a moment while I lock all the doors and windows?

4. The police decided to wait _____ the thieves hiding in the bushes.

5. A lack of funding held _____ completion of the project for several weeks.

6. Even though most employees signed the petition asking for salary increases, the boss just _____ on the matter for months.

7. The Crandalls killed _____ waiting for their flight by reading the newspaper.

8. I'm sorry, but Mrs. Nielsen is unavailable until this afternoon because she's all _____ up with interviews this morning.

9. Why did the boss call off the meeting instead of putting it _____ until he returns from the business trip?

B. Choose the statement in the right column that best responds to the question in the left column. Write the appropriate number in the blank.

NOTE: *To do this as a listening exercise, cover up the left column before you start the tape.*

1. Has the staff meeting for today been called off?

2. What's holding up traffic ahead of us on the highway?

3. Would you like me to hold on while you answer the phone?

4. Are flights running late because of the storm?

5. Can we put this proposal on the back burner?

____ a. They must be. We can kill time by visiting the gift shop.

____ b. Yes, we can, if we choose just to sit on it.

____ c. I don't know. If it's an accident, we'll just have to wait it out.

____ d. No, it's just been put off until next week.

____ e. Thanks a lot. I'll be with you in just a moment.

C. Use the idioms in your spoken or written answers to the following questions.

1. What are some different ways to *kill time* on a long driving or flying trip?

2. What are some possible reasons why someone would *be running late* for work?

3. Are you a patient person who can *wait* something *out*, or are you generally impatient? Why?

4. Why would a responsible person choose to *sit on* a matter instead of making a decision?

5. Do you ever get *tied up* and have to miss a class or appointment? What do you do?

D. Using the idioms from this unit, develop a dialogue or role play about a situation that causes you a delay and requires you to be patient. You may include the following information:

- what or who holds you up;
- whether you are running late as a result;
- how you kill time while you're waiting;
- whether it's necessary to call or put something off.

Unit 44
Interfering and Disturbing

be in the way   to be in a position to interfere or block progress
also: **get in the way**

USAGE NOTE: Possessive adjectives such as *my* and *your* can be used instead of *the*.

■ Why *are* you always *in the way* when I'm trying to cook dinner?
■ The children wanted to help us paint the house, but actually they just *got in our way.*

stick one's nose into   to interfere purposely
also: **butt in(to)**
related idiom: **step in(to)** to interfere with the purpose of being helpful
USAGE NOTE: *Butt in* is more informal than *stick one's nose into*.

■ Whenever Dale's mother-in-law comes to visit, she always *sticks her nose into* everything.
■ Why do you *butt in* every time I'm trying to have a serious discussion with Dad?
■ When Timmy and Billy started fighting, their parents had to *step in* to prevent one of the boys from getting hurt.

busy-body   someone who interferes in the affairs of others, a nosey person
GRAMMAR NOTE: This idiom is spelled as one word in some dictionaries.

■ My neighbor is always asking questions about our family. She's such a *busy-body.*
■ If you weren't a *busy-body*, you'd have more time to solve your own problems.

get on someone's case   to put pressure on someone (often by criticizing)
also: **get on someone's back**
opposite meaning: **get off someone's case, get off someone's back**

■ Tom's parents are always *getting on his case* to find a steady job and to be more independent of them.
■ I don't need you to keep reminding me to lose weight. Just *get off my back!*

be none of someone's business   not to be of concern to someone

■ Where I go and what I do *is none of your business* anymore, Mom.
■ I know it*'s none of my business*, but should you be partying so much and neglecting your studies?

mind one's own business   to concern oneself with one's own affairs and not the affairs of others

also: **keep (one's nose) out of, butt out**

USAGE NOTE: The idiom *butt out* should be used informally.

■ Would you please *mind your own business?* I'd rather do this by myself.

■ Earl has learned to simplify life by *keeping his nose out of* other people's business.

■ This matter is no concern of yours. *Butt out!*

knock it off   to stop doing something that bothers someone else

also: **cut it out, leave someone alone**

GRAMMAR NOTE: These idioms are separable, but only *leave alone* takes a noun or pronoun other than *it*.

■ Boys, you're making too much noise in the house. *Knock it off!*

■ *Cut it out*, Angie. You know how I hate to be tickled like that.

■ Robbie is trying to get his work done, so please *leave* him *alone*.

go away   to leave someone who has been bothered

also: **get lost, take a hike**

USAGE NOTE: The alternate forms are quite informal.

■ How many times have I told you that I need peace and quiet to study? Please *go away* and leave me alone!

■ Cynthia told Mitch to *get lost* when he appeared at her door again for no special reason.

■ If you're going to keep criticizing this TV program I'm watching, *take a hike!*

EXERCISES

A.   **Fill in each blank with the missing part of the idiom.**

1. Stop asking me those questions. It's _____ of your business.

2. Laura's father always _____ on her case about the way she dresses.

3. My landlord is such a _____-body. She always seems to know when I come and go.

4. Why are you teasing your brother like that? _____ it off right now!

5. Why does the boss have to _____ his nose into our personal affairs?

6. You have no right to tell me what to do. Why don't you _____ your own business?

7. If you don't go _____ right now, I'll tell Dad that you're bothering me.

8. Johnny, I'm trying to clean the house and you're just in the _____. Please go outside and play.

B. Choose the statement in the right column that best responds to the question in the left column. Write the appropriate number in the blank.

NOTE: *To do this as a listening exercise, cover up the left column before you start the tape.*

1. Mom, could you tell him to leave me alone?
2. Why do you keep getting on my case about paying the rent?
3. Why do you think that your roommate is a busy-body?
4. Could you please step to one side? You're in the way.
5. How many times have I told you to take a hike?

____ a. I'll get off your case when you have money to share expenses.

____ b. Oh, she keeps sticking her nose into my private business.

____ c. I'm sorry. I didn't mean to get in your way.

____ d. As many times as you've told me to get lost!

____ e. Mikey, cut it out right now.

C. Use the idioms in your spoken or written answers to the following questions.

1. Do you know anyone who is a **busy-body?** How do you feel about this person?
2. At what point should a parent **keep his or her nose out of** a child's business?
3. Do your parents ever try to **step in** and tell you what to do? How do you respond?
4. Why might a wife **get on her husband's case?** Why might a husband **get on his wife's case?**
5. **Is** anyone or anything **in the way** of your achieving your goals in life? Who or what has **gotten in your way?**

D. Using the idioms from this unit, develop a dialogue or role play about someone who keeps disturbing you or interfering in your affairs. You may include the following information:

- whether or not this person is generally a busy-body;
- what this person does to butt into your affairs;
- why you think that your affairs are none of this person's business;
- how you tell this person to leave you alone;
- whether or not this person finally gets off your case.

139

Unit 45
Needs, Wants, and Preferences

have got to   must, to have an obligation to
also: **have to**

- Look at the time. It's getting late. I**'ve got to** go.

- **Haven't** you **got to** leave now if you're going to get there on time?

- Mrs. Lewis **has to** meet with her son's teacher to discuss his performance.

had better   should, to be advisable to
also: **ought to**

GRAMMAR NOTE: *Had* often occurs in contracted form (*'d*).

- Elizabeth **had better** change her attitude or she'll upset her boss even more.

- Don't you think you**'d better** go to bed before you fall asleep on the couch?

- You **ought to** visit the doctor before your condition worsens.

be supposed to   to be expected to

- You**'re supposed** to wash the dirt from your socks before putting them in the washing machine.

- **Isn't** Mike **supposed to** be here already? I wonder what happened to him.

feel like   to desire to, to want to

GRAMMAR NOTE: This idiom is often followed by a gerund (verb + *-ing*).

- I **feel like** cooking dinner on the barbecue tonight. We haven't done that in a long time.

- Don't you **feel like** a nice cold glass of water after you exercise?

long for   to desire greatly (in the sense of missing something)
also: **die for, be itching to**

GRAMMAR NOTE: *Long for* and *die for* are often used in a continuous verb tense, while *be itching to* always is.

- Jeff and Pauline are **longing for** a family, but they realize they have to wait a few years until their careers are well established.

- Wouldn't you **die for** a nice cup of coffee right now?

- After her wonderful trip to Europe last year, Esther **is itching to** return.

could do with   to enjoy, to benefit from
also: **could go for**
- After that strenuous yard work, I **could do with** a cold drink.
- The stereo is on very loud. **Couldn't** you **do with** more peace and quiet?
- I'm so tired I sure **could go for** a short nap now.

would rather   to prefer
also: **would just as soon**
GRAMMAR NOTE: *Would* often occurs in contracted form (*'d*).
- Unlike most people, Karla **would rather** go to work than take a vacation.
- Bill said he**'d rather** handle the Alston negotiations personally.
- Actually, I**'d just as soon** stay home for dinner than eat out at a restaurant.

so much the better   an exclamation that shows preference for a situation
- I play racquetball for the fun and exercise, but if I happen to win, **so much the better.**
- JOAN: My curried rice dish is spicier than usual.
  BEN: **So much the better!**

to each one's own   each person has his or her own preference
USAGE NOTE: This expression is usually used with the male possessive adjective *his*.
- Albert has strange taste in clothes, but as I always say, **to each his own!**
- LEIGH: Can you believe that Millie would rather stay home alone than to go out with friends?
  DOUG: **To each his own!**

have got dibs on   to have reserved for oneself
- I**'ve got dibs on** the biggest piece of pie because I've got the largest stomach!
- Can't you see that we**'ve got dibs** on these seats? That's why we put our jackets there.

EXERCISES

A. Fill in each blank with the missing part of the idiom.

EVE: Will, hadn't you ＿＿＿＿＿＿＿ do some chores around the house today?
        ₁

WILL: I sure don't feel ＿＿＿＿＿＿＿ doing any. I would ＿＿＿＿＿＿＿ just
                        ₂   ₃
       sit here and watch football.

EVE: Remember our agreement? You're only ＿＿＿＿＿＿＿ to watch football
                                           ₄
      when your favorite team is playing.

WILL: OK, OK, I guess I could ＿＿＿＿＿＿＿ with less TV. But you've
                               ₅
       ＿＿＿＿＿＿＿ to help me with the chores.
       ₆

EVE: I know. I've got ＿＿＿＿＿＿＿ on the kitchen.
                       ₇

WILL: Since I'd rather clean up the living room, so ＿＿＿＿＿＿＿ the better!
                                                     ₈

EVE: (Later, after some chores are done) I could ＿＿＿＿＿＿＿ with a break
                                                  ₉
      about now.

Will: Me too. I'm longing _____ for some more football.
$$\overline{10}$$

Eve: Well, there's no harm in watching the end of the game, I guess.

Will: Thanks!

B.   **Choose the statement in the right column that best responds to the question in the left column. Write the appropriate number in the blank.**

NOTE: *To do this as a listening exercise, cover up the left column before you start the tape.*

1. Wouldn't you rather finish watching this movie?

2. Didn't Tim say that over 200 people are supposed to come to the party?

3. Is there anything you've got to do this afternoon?

4. Aren't you dying for some soda right now?

5. Who's got dibs on the last piece of chocolate cake?

____ a. Not really, but I could go for a cold glass of water.

____ b. Yes, I have to wash and vacuum the car.

____ c. No, I'd just as soon switch to the news.

____ d. You'd better let Meg have it, since it's her birthday!

____ e. Is that right? So much the better!

C.   **Use the idioms in your spoken or written answers to the following questions.**

1. If someone is overweight, what *had* they *better* do?
2. What *would* you *rather* do than work for a living?
3. Is there anything in the world you*'re itching to* see or do? What?
4. Do you ever *feel like* taking a nap during the day? When?
5. In what situation could you say, *"To each his own"?* Why?

D.   **Using the idioms from this unit, develop a dialogue or role play about a group of friends who are trying to decide what they want to do together. You may include the following information:**

- what each person feels like doing;
- what you would rather do, if different from the others;
- whether you'd better hurry to decide;
- whether anyone has got to do a chore or task instead;
- whether anyone is itching to get started immediately.

Unit 46
Interest and Disinterest

take an interest in　to be interested in
> also: **go in for**
>
> USAGE NOTE: *Go in for* is usually used for interest in hobbies or sports.
>
> ■ Parents who ***take an interest in*** their children's education are well aware of the potential benefits.
> ■ My wife ***goes in for*** reading and playing cards while I ***go in for*** tennis and soccer.

be into　to have as a hobby or sport, to spend a lot of time doing
> also: **be hooked on, get into**
>
> ■ Mr. Evans *is* really ***into*** woodworking. He makes all his own furniture!
> ■ I'***m hooked on*** physical exercise. Unless I do it three times a week, I don't feel right.
> ■ Have you ***gotten into*** snowboarding yet? I think it's a wonderful sport.

take up　to start, to undertake
> GRAMMAR/USAGE NOTES: The idiom is separable and is used when someone starts a new sport, hobby, or even a career.
>
> ■ Mrs. Sinclair was advised to ***take up*** walking as a way to strengthen her muscles.
> ■ Jason ***took*** stamp collecting ***up*** when he inherited his grandfather's collection.
> ■ It's never too late to ***take up*** a new occupation if you really want to.

take to　to find appealing or interesting
> ■ Emily didn't have any trouble learning to swim. She ***took to*** water like a fish.
> ■ Stephen didn't need convincing about the importance of computers. He ***took to*** them very quickly.

to one's heart's content　as much as one wishes
> ■ Sandy and Nina love to go to nightclubs and dance ***to their heart's content.***
> ■ Once a week Felicia forgets her diet and eats dessert ***to her heart's content.***

look forward to　to anticipate with pleasure
> GRAMMAR NOTE: This idiom is often followed by a gerund (verb + -*ing*).
>
> ■ It's still four months away, but I'm really ***looking forward to*** going on vacation.
> ■ Aren't you ***looking forward to*** your big date with Connie?

get a kick out of   to enjoy greatly

GRAMMAR NOTE: This expression is usually followed by a gerund (verb + -ing).

■ Old Grandpa Anderson *gets a kick out of* watching his grandchildren play sports.

■ I *get a kick out of* getting up early to watch a pretty sunrise over the mountains.

turn off   to give a bad impression or feeling to someone
also: **leave someone cold**

GRAMMAR NOTE: These expressions are usually separated.

■ Body odor and smelly clothing always *turn* me *off.*

■ Nate wishes that he enjoyed classical music, but unfortunately it just *leaves* him *cold.*

put to sleep   to bore, not to interest at all

GRAMMAR NOTE: An object always follows the verb.

■ How can you watch that long TV documentary show? It's *putting* me *to sleep.*

■ The lecturer *put* the audience *to sleep* with his relaxed, slow style of speech.

old hat   something that is not new or original

■ Violence in American movies and TV programs is rapidly becoming *old hat.*

■ I've been listening to jazz all my life, so it's *old hat* to me.

EXERCISES

A.   **Fill in each blank with the missing part of the idiom.**

1. I don't watch television very much anymore because most of the shows are _____ hat.

2. That boring lecture really put me to _____. How about you?

3. A pass to Disneyland allows you to ride all of the attractions to your heart's _____.

4. Didn't you get a _____ out of riding the Ferris wheel at the amusement park?

5. The Derns are looking _____ to a visit from their grandchildren.

6. I didn't know that Alba had _____ up aerobics recently.

7. Keith is really _____ Zen philosophy. He meditates nearly every day.

8. Mr. Tripp didn't take an _____ in old cars until he retired.

9. The tennis champion _____ to swinging a racquet at the age of six.

10. People who don't listen really _____ Jill off.

B. Choose the statement in the right column that best responds to the question in the left column. Write the appropriate number in the blank.

NOTE: *To do this as a listening exercise, cover up the left column before you start the tape.*

1. Have you ever taken an interest in the ballet?

2. When did Larry take up skydiving?

3. Don't you get a kick out of watching the kids play together?

4. You're really into using your computer to explore the Internet, aren't you?

5. Does the smell of curried rice turn you off?

____ a. Yes, it's true—Indian food leaves me cold.

____ b. Not really. That kind of dancing puts me to sleep.

____ c. Yes, and here in the park they can run to their heart's content.

____ d. Into it? I'm hooked on it!

____ e. He got into it a couple of months ago.

C. Use the idioms in your spoken or written answers to the following questions.

1. When did you first **take an interest in** learning English? **Are** you still **into** it?

2. Have you **taken to** using computers? Why or why not?

3. Why do some people **get a kick out of** riding rollercoasters? Do you? Why or why not?

4. What are some unusual hobbies that people **take up?**

5. What kinds of things **turn** you **off?**

D. Using the idioms from this unit, tell a classmate about your past and present interests. You may include the following information:

- what you got into as a child, and whether you still go in for it now;
- what you love to do to your heart's content;
- what puts you to sleep;
- whether you're really into learning English, or whether it's old hat to you;
- what you'd like to take up in the future.

Unit 47
Certainty and Doubt

make sure   to determine something to be true
also: **make certain**

- Sema *made sure* that she had enough money in her checking account to buy the stereo.
- Why don't you *make certain* that you locked the garage after you parked the car?

for sure   certainly, definitely

- I'll pick you up at the airport by five o'clock *for sure.*
- Artie said *for sure* he'd be over later to help us.

(there are) no ifs, ands, or buts about it   (it's) absolutely certain
also: **beyond (a shadow of) a doubt**

- You will tell your father about the accident, and *there are not ifs, ands, or buts about it.*
- This is the best steak I've ever eaten—*no ifs, ands, or buts about it.*
- *Beyond a shadow of a doub*t, this is the most relaxing vacation we've had in a long time.

mark my words   about this, I am certain

GRAMMAR/USAGE NOTES: This idiom usually starts a sentence, and is used when someone feels certain about what will happen in the future.

- *Mark my words*, I'll never smoke another cigarette again as long as I live.
- Shirley will never get a promotion after that stupid mistake she made, *mark my words.*

bet on it   to be guaranteed by someone, to be certain about

USAGE NOTE: The auxiliary *can* often precedes this expression.

- Do you really think that Jack will do it? Don't *bet on it!*
- TARA: Will we see you at the party Friday night?
  MIKE: You can *bet on it!*

believe in   to trust, to have faith in

- It's important for children to *believe in* their parents as good role models.
- Throughout history, some cultures have *believed in* one god, while other cultures have *believed in* the existence of many gods.

take at someone's word   to accept or believe someone's promise

GRAMMAR NOTE: This idiom must be separated by an object following the verb.

- When Todd said he'd repay the $100 within a week, I *took* him *at his word.*
- Vera *took* Trey *at his word* when he promised never to borrow her car without permission again.

take someone's word for it   to accept what someone says as true

- I didn't see you hit the ball over the fence, but I'll *take your word for it.*
- Garrett *took my word for it* that he'd mistakenly left the door unlocked when he left.

give the benefit of the doubt   to believe someone until there is clear proof of an error or a lie

GRAMMAR NOTE: This expression is separated by an object.

- Why don't you *give* Leah *the benefit of the doubt* instead of assuming it's her mistake?
- Frank denies stealing, but I can't prove it, so I'll have to *give* him *the benefit of the doubt.*

Give me a break   Don't expect me to believe

also: **Come off it, Come on, Spare me, Don't give me that**

USAGE NOTE: These expressions are almost always used in the first person. *Come on* can be combined with all the other forms except *come off it.*

- It's the teacher's fault that you got a *D* on your test? *Give me a break!*
- You didn't know you were driving 80 miles per hour? *Come on, don't give me that!*
- You always have a good excuse for avoiding your responsibilities, so *spare me* this time.

EXERCISES

A.   **Fill in each blank with the missing part of the idiom.**

1. Mark my _____, there will be a computer in every household within the next decade.

2. John said that he'd _____ sure that Bruce got my note.

3. Barbara probably cheated, but we've got to give her the _____ of the doubt if we can't prove it.

4. I'll take your _____ for it that Jean has a good excuse for having lost the artwork.

5. It's impossible to believe _____ the integrity of a politician who has been arrested for bribery and theft.

6. When I asked Ted if I could depend on his help, he said that I could bet _____ it.

7. The package of materials you ordered will be mailed today for _____.

8. Chris will pay for her mistake, and there are no ifs, _____, or buts about it.

9. You're trying to tell me that you're late because you had another flat tire? Give me a _____!

10. You shouldn't _____ Kevin at his word. He often fails to do what he promises.

B. Choose the statement in the right column that best responds to the question in the left column. Write the appropriate number in the blank.

NOTE: *To do this as a listening exercise, cover up the left column before you start the tape.*

1. I heard a noise. Could you make sure that no one entered the house?

2. Did you take Denise's word for it that she didn't take the missing folder?

3. Do you think that the witness is telling the truth beyond a shadow of a doubt?

4. Can I take you at your word that you'll repay the fifty dollars soon?

5. Did Vicki make certain that our team plays at nine o'clock in the morning?

____ a. He's under oath, so I have to believe in his testimony.

____ b. Come on! I didn't hear a sound. You're imagining things.

____ c. You'll have it tomorrow. You can bet on it!

____ d. Yes, she did, and mark my words—we're going to win!

____ e. Without proof, I have to give her the benefit of the doubt.

C. Use the idioms in your spoken or written answers to the following questions.

1. Do you *make certain* to lock all the doors and windows in your home before you go to bed? Why or why not?

2. Is there anything in life that you know *for sure* will happen? What?

3. If someone told you that they had seen a U.F.O. (Unidentifed Flying Object, or vehicle for space travel), would you tell them to *come off it?* Why or why not?

4. Some people think that killing another person is always wrong—*no ifs, ands, or buts about it.* What do you think?

5. Some people believe that human beings developed by natural evolution, while others believe that a god or "spirit" created human beings. Which do you *believe in?* Why?

D. Using the idioms from this unit, develop a dialogue or role play about an event that someone claimed happened, but that you doubt actually happened. You may include the following information:

- what the person claims happened;
- for what reasons you don't take the person at his or her word;
- what expression you use to show your disbelief;
- how the person indicates that you should believe in what he or she says;
- whether or not you finally give the person the benefit of the doubt;
- whether there's any way to make sure that what the person says is true.

Unit 48
Approval and Disapproval

be in favor of   to approve of, to support
- All of you who *are in favor of* the proposal, please raise your hands.
- Would you *be in favor of* remodeling the kitchen so we can have a breakfast nook?

give the green light   to approve of, to give permission
also: **give the go-ahead**

GRAMMAR NOTE: These idioms are separable, but an object is not necessary.
- The boss *gave the green light* for the company to start a new advertising campaign.
- If you *give* me *the go-ahead*, I'll visit the travel agency tomorrow to make reservations.

a big hand   approval in the form of applause
- At the end of the wonderful performance, the audience gave the pianist *a big hand*.
- I think Ahmed deserves *a big hand* for a very thorough report on his country.

sound good   to meet with one's approval
also: **sound great**
- A nice home-cooked meal and a video *sound good* to me.
- You're going to get me a bicycle for my birthday? That *sounds great!*

go ahead   to give permission to proceed or continue
also: **be my guest, feel free to**
- I'm not ready to eat yet, but you can *go ahead*.
- AUNT: Can I play your piano a little?
  NIECE: Sure, *be my guest*.
- *Feel free to* grab something from the refrigerator if you're thirsty.

shake one's head   to show disapproval by moving the head from side to side
- When Patrick told his dad that he wasn't planning to go to college, his dad just *shook his head* and left the room quietly.
- Whenever I see newborn infants already drinking formula milk, I can only *shake my head*.

take a dim view of   to disapprove of
- Sonya's parents *take a dim view of* her wearing cosmetics at the age of ten.
- Most Americans would *take a dim view of* any plan to increase income taxes.

149

give a dirty look   to show disapproval by looking at someone with an expression
of resentment

GRAMMAR NOTE: This idiom is separable, but an object is not necessary.

- When I told my son that he had to help me with yardwork, he just *gave a dirty look.*
- Why did you *give* Emmanuelle *a dirty look* like that? It's not her fault!

I'm afraid not   No, Never
also: **Forget it, No way**

- SON: Can Danny stay at our house tonight, Dad?
  DAD: *I'm afraid not*, son.
- SAM: Can I borrow ten dollars, Ed?
  ED: *Forget it*, Sam.
- You want me to go skydiving with you some day? *No way!*

be out of the question   to be impossible, not to be practical
also: **over one's dead body**

- It*'s out of the question* for you to travel to Disney World alone.
- DAUGHTER: Could I have a party while you're gone?
  PARENT: That*'s out of the question.*
- You'll smoke inside this house *over my dead body!*

EXERCISES

A.   **Fill in each blank with the missing part of the idiom.**

NED: This is a wonderful talk. The speaker surely deserves a big _____.
$_1$

SUE: Go _____ and applaud if you want to. I won't.
$_2$

NED: Why are you shaking your _____ at me like that?
$_3$

SUE: You know that I take a dim _____ of simple solutions to complicated
$_4$

problems. Giving the _____ light to more prisons is not the right
$_5$

answer.

NED: Aren't you in _____ of putting criminals in jail for a long time?
$_6$

SUE: I'm _____ not. That idea _____ good on the surface, but it
$_7$ $_8$

really doesn't solve the crime problem.

NED: How can you say that? Isn't it out of the _____ to leave these
$_9$

criminals on the streets?

SUE: Of course, but there must be alternatives to the present system. All prison does
is to make criminals more dangerous than ever!

NED: We shouldn't talk anymore. The person sitting next to you is giving us a
_____ look!
$_{10}$

B. Choose the statement in the right column that best responds to the question in the left column. Write the appropriate number in the blank.

NOTE: *To do this as a listening exercise, cover up the left column before you start the tape.*

1. Can I get something to eat from your refrigerator?

____ a. Yes, I was so happy when he gave us the green light.

2. Did Mr. Larsen give you the go-ahead on the business deal?

____ b. I have no objection if you're in favor of it.

3. Is it out of the question for Billy to have his friends sleep here overnight?

____ c. She just shook her head and left.

4. What did Sharon say when you informed her of our decision?

____ d. No way. I take a dim view of all his ideas.

5. Did you join the audience in giving the guest lecturer a big hand?

____ e. Sure, be my guest.

C. Use the idioms in your spoken or written answers to the following questions.

1. Have you ever received *a big hand* for doing something special? What?
2. What kind of food *sounds good* to you right now?
3. Do you ever *give* someone *a dirty look?* When?
4. Would you *give the go-ahead* to a law that would make cigarette smoking illegal? Why or why not?
5. *Are* you *in favor of* legalizing some drugs for medicinal purposes? Why or why not?

D. Using the idioms from this unit, develop a presentation describing how your opinion of capital punishment differs from the opinion of a friend or classmate. You may include the following information:

- whether either or both of you are in favor of capital punishment, and why;
- whether either or both of you take a dim view of it, and why;
- whether capital punishment has been given a green light in your country, or
- whether it's still out of the question.

Unit 49
Self-Control

get (a)hold of oneself to regain self-control
    also: **get a grip on oneself**

Usage Note: This idiom is used when someone is already losing self-control. *Keep* can be used instead of *get.*

- There's no reason to be so upset. ***Get ahold of yourself!***
- I told Hermes to ***get a grip on himself*** or his parents would notice his nervousness.
- If they'd ***kept a grip on*** themselves, the argument wouldn't have happened.

keep one's wits (about one) to remain alert and in control

- Our team ***kept its wits*** and was able to score three quick goals to win.
- The lost boy ***kept his wits about him*** and found his way to the nearest police station.

keep one's cool to stay calm, to stay in control
    also: **keep one's head**
    opposite meaning: **lose one's cool, lose one's head, get carried away**

- Most of the guests ***kept their cool*** when a fire alarm sounded accidentally.
- In any situation it's better to ***keep your head*** than to ***get carried away.***
- It's not like Ellen to ***lose her cool*** like that.
- When Steve insulted me, I ***lost my head*** and said things I didn't mean.

have one's act together to have full control of one's life
    also: **get one's act together**

- Charlene is a successful lawyer, mother, and wife. She really ***has her act together.***
- If I want to pass all my courses this semester, I'd better ***get my act together.***

mind over matter the power of the mind over physical matters

- Taking a very cold shower is just a question of ***mind over matter.***
- Practitioners of alternative medicine believe that diseases can be cured by ***mind over matter.***

level-headed sensible, having common sense

- The office workers appreciate Mrs. Diamond because she's such a ***level-headed*** manager.
- Why does Arthur always have to be so ***level-headed?*** Can't he do anything spontaneously?

on the ball   alert and competent
also: **on one's toes**
USAGE NOTE: These expressions are often used with the verbs *keep* and *stay.*
■ The lifeguard was really **on the ball** when he saw someone far out at sea waving their arms.
■ If you go downtown at night, you'd better keep **on your toes**, because it's dangerous.
■ Carla stayed **on the ball** while fixing a leak on the edge of the roof.

hold in(side)   to keep emotions inside, to fail to express
opposite meaning: **let out**
■ Mr. Baxter started to show his annoyance, but instead **held** it **in**.
■ It may generally be better to **let** your feelings **out** than to **hold** them **inside.**

EXERCISES

A.   **Fill in each blank with the missing part of the idiom.**

1. How did you notice that mistake? You're really on the _____.

2. The police remained _____-headed during the serious emergency.

3. The water in the swimming pool isn't too cold. Just use _____ over matter!

4. Maxine was able to _____ her cool when confronting her boss about her low salary.

5. The boy kept his _____ about him after falling into the fast-moving river.

6. Drew has a fine career and wonderful family. He really has his act _____.

7. Mr. Montanez felt very emotional as he struggled to _____ the tears in.

8. Why are you becoming so angry? _____ ahold of yourself!

B.   **Choose the statement in the right column that best responds to the question in the left column. Write the appropriate number in the blank.**

NOTE: *To do this as a listening exercise, cover up the left column before you start the tape.*

1. I've never seen Blake lose his cool. How does he do it?

2. How did you manage to get your act together and lose weight so quickly?

3. Why doesn't Heather share her feelings instead of holding them inside?

4. Wasn't Mr. Okamura really on the ball when he saved that young girl?

5. Why did the boss get carried away by shouting at her assistant?

____ a. If he hadn't been on his toes, the child would be dead now.

____ b. He just knows how to keep his wits about him.

____ c. It was mind over matter that solved my problem.

____ d. Good question. She just can't seem to let them out.

____ e. I don't know, but it wasn't a level-headed way to act.

C. Use the idioms in your spoken or written answers to the following questions.

1. Is it generally better to *let* your feelings *out* or to *hold* them *inside?* If possible, explain why.
2. Have you ever been in a situation where you had to *get ahold of yourself?* When?
3. Give some examples of how a person could use *mind over matter.*
4. Why does a police officer have to be *on the ball?* When do you have to be *on your toes?*
5. What are some signs that people don't *have their act together?* How can people *get their act together* when they have serious problems?

D. Using the idioms from this unit, tell a classmate about a situation where you showed self-control. You may include the following information:

- whether you're generally a level-headed person;
- whether it's natural for you to be on your toes at all times;
- the situation in which you had to keep your cool;
- how you were able to keep your head;
- whether you had to get a grip on yourself at any point;
- which of your friends or family members were also involved and whether they showed self-control like you.

Unit 50
Success and Failure

get ahead   to succeed in life, to advance
> also: **go far, make good**
- You can't *get ahead* in life if you're always lazy and waste money like that!
- Bettina is such a hard worker that I'm sure she'll *go far* in the world.
- Everyone was surprised when slow Bruno *made good* as a professional boxer.

make the grade   to succeed in meeting certain requirements or standards
- Westin was cut from the college baseball team because he couldn't *make the grade.*

pull off   to succeed in causing to happen, to accomplish
> also: **bring off, carry off**

USAGE NOTE: These idioms are separable, and are used when success is not really expected.
- Carlton *pulled off* a small miracle when he convinced his parents to buy him a car.
- If anyone can *bring off* the huge ten-band concert, West Coast Productions can.
- When the central bank was robbed, the police wondered how the criminals *carried* it *off.*

make it big   to achieve great personal and financial success
> also: **make it to the big time**
- Richard *made it big* in the real estate market by buying cheap properties and making them profitable.
- Actor Warren Price *made it to the big time* when he was given his own TV show.

come back   to succeed in regaining one's previous high status or position
> also: **make a comeback**
- After years of personal struggle, Anne has managed to *come back* and continue her singing career.
- Todd still thinks he can *make a comeback* in football after his terrible knee injury.

go over   to succeed in gaining the appreciation of others
- Judging from the applause, I think my speech *went over* well.
- The comedian knew from the audience's reaction that his jokes weren't *going over* well.

blow it   to fail badly, to make a serious mistake

- That aptitude test wasn't very difficult. How did you manage to **blow it?**
- I really **blew it** when I declined to go on the camping trip. I heard it was great.

give up   to admit failure, to stop trying
also: **throw in the towel**

- Can you get this door to unlock? I **give up!**
- You still have time to finish your research paper. Don't **throw in the towel** yet!

in vain   without success, for no useful purpose
also: **for nothing**

- The paramedics tried **in vain** to revive the drowning victim.
- There was no exam today, so I did all that studying last night **for nothing!**

lost cause   a person or thing that has failed and cannot probably be saved

- I'm afraid that Sydney is so addicted to drugs and alcohol that he's a **lost cause.**
- Harriet's old car has over 200,000 miles on it, so it's nearly a **lost cause.**
- I guess my proposal is a **lost cause** because no one else on the committee agrees with it.

back to square one   starting at the beginning again
also: **back to the drawing board**

- Thirty minutes on this physics problem and we still didn't do it correctly. It's **back to square one!**
- The military attack failed badly, so the generals had to go **back to the drawing board.**

EXERCISES

A.   **Fill in each blank with the missing part of the idiom.**

1. Gail was sure that she could make the _____ at the Naval Academy and become an officer.

2. One way to get _____ in life is to use self-control and make the necessary effort.

3. The architects had to go back to _____ one when the owners didn't approve their building design.

4. A person who gives _____ easily is one who can't see the rewards of success.

5. I forgot to mail this important letter today. I really _____ it!

6. The firefighters tried to save the burning car, but it quickly became a _____ cause.

7. Effort made to correct a wrongful situation, even if it fails, is not made in _____.

8. All of the actor's friends thought he was too old to _____ back in films, but he proved them all wrong.

9. Some day Mr. Burton is going to make it _____ in the fashion world.

10. If you can get Valerie to come with us, you'll have pulled _____ a miracle.

11. The manager's suggestion to reduce hours of operation didn't _____ over well among the employees.

B. Choose the statement in the right column that best responds to the question in the left column. Write the appropriate number in the blank.

NOTE: *To do this as a listening exercise, cover up the left column before you start the tape.*

1. Are you saying that this project didn't make the grade with the boss?

2. Does Fred really think that he can make a comeback in baseball?

3. Did your third marriage proposal to Annette go over better than the others?

4. Why did Mrs. James throw in the towel and close her business?

5. Don't you think that Jody will go far in politics?

____ a. Because her efforts to get a loan to save it were in vain.

____ b. No, I finally realize that trying to convince her is a lost cause.

____ c. Maybe, if she doesn't promise too much and then blow it!

____ d. Yes, I'm afraid that it's back to the drawing board.

____ e. Yes, and he thinks that he'll make it to the big time again!

C. Use the idioms in your spoken or written answers to the following questions.

1. What are some ways to **get ahead** in life? Is **making good** in life important to you?

2. Are you someone who easily **throws in the towel** in a difficult situation, or do you try to **bring** it **off?**

3. If you were a candidate for president of the United States, what qualifications would you have to meet in order to **make the grade** with the citizens?

4. What are some reasons why an older athlete might try to **make a comeback** in sports?

5. If there was something in life that you would like to **bring off**, what would it be?

D. Using the idioms from this unit, develop a dialogue or role play about a discussion between you and your friends on successes and failures in life. You may include the following information:

- how you've managed to get ahead in life;
- whether anyone had made it big or is close to doing so;
- whether anyone has made a lot of effort in vain;
- whether anyone tried to carry something off but then had to throw in the towel;
- whether anyone once was a lost cause but then made a comeback.

Review: Units 41–50

A. Circle the expression that best completes each sentence.

1. Mrs. Lane is really _____ the day that she can retire and take up a new hobby.
   a. looking forward to
   b. giving the green light to
   c. giving up

2. Would you mind _____ a moment? I have to feed the cats before we leave.
   a. hanging up
   b. holding on
   c. waiting out

3. Mehmet has on a long face because he studied for the exam _____. He really blew it.
   a. in high spirits
   b. to each his own
   c. in vain

4. My daughter gave me a dirty look when I said that buying her a new car was _____.
   a. taking her at her word
   b. making a comeback
   c. out of the question

5. Isabel _____ get a grip on herself if she doesn't want to blow her stack.
   a. had better
   b. would rather
   c. sounds good to

6. You're supposed to mind your own business, and there's _____.
   a. killing time
   b. put it on the back burner
   c. no ifs, ands, or buts about it

7. Beautiful weather and a walk in the park really _____.
   a. made my day
   b. was a happy camper
   c. turned me off

8. Why don't you _____ and leave without me? I don't want to hold you up.
   a. sit on it
   b. go ahead
   c. put it off

9. If Aaron can _____ this big business deal, he'll really get ahead in the company.
   a. storm out of
   b. die for
   c. pull off

10. Why don't you _____ tennis like me? Then we could play together.
    a. turn on
    b. take up
    c. take a dim view of

B. Indicate whether each statement is TRUE (T) or FALSE (F).

_____ 1. A busy-body is someone who takes an interest in other peoples' lives.

_____ 2. A task that you've got to do every day might become a pain in the neck.

_____ 3. You'd feel blue if you were floating on cloud nine.

_____ 4. Someone might tell you to get lost if you're sticking your nose into their business.

_____ 5. If you're always running late to work, then you're on the ball.

_____ 6. Someone who kept their cool probably wouldn't raise their voice.

_____ 7. Blowing off steam is one way of letting anger out.

_____ 8. Someone who made the grade has his or her act together.

_____ 9. Something that puts you to sleep would lift your spirits.

_____ 10. You're back to square one if you manage to pull something off.

C. Complete the puzzle with the missing parts of the idioms in the sentences below.

ACROSS

3. That movie was a real tear-_____.
5. Don't throw in the _____ yet.
6. It's none of your _____ what I do.
7. Eat dessert to your heart's _____.
10. Hard work can get you _____ in life.
11. Don't hit the _____ when I tell you the bad news.

DOWN

1. Losing weight is a question of mind over _____.
2. My new wife and I are still in seventh _____.
4. The exam is postponed? So I studied for _____.
6. If your friends are coming too, so much the _____.
7. The sound of birds outside our bedroom drives us _____.
8. You're not supposed to tease me. _____ it off!
9. The audience gave the performer a big _____.

Index

Answer Key

Unit 1
Exercise A
1. wink
2. go
3. crack
4. up
5. sleeps
6. take
7. in
8. get
9. off
10. ready

Exercise B
a. 3
b. 5
c. 1
d. 2
e. 4

Unit 2
Exercise A
1. out
2. stayed
3. hours
4. hit
5. out
6. fell
7. up
8. turned
9. down

Exercise B
a. 5
b. 1
c. 4
d. 2
e. 3

Unit 3
Exercise A
1. clean
2. up
3. fix
4. dishes
5. take
6. house
7. sales
8. fix
9. odds
10. put

Exercise B
a. 3
b. 4
c. 5
d. 2
e. 1

Unit 4
Exercise A
1. call
2. in
3. in
4. living
5. collar
6. do
7. closes
8. get
9. shift

Exercise B
a. 3
b. 5
c. 1
d. 2
e. 4

Unit 5
Exercise A
1. off
2. see
3. check
4. leave
5. booked
6. get
7. away
8. out
9. take/soak

Exercise B
a. 5
b. 3
c. 1
d. 4
e. 2

Unit 6
Exercise A
1. take
2. loosen
3. passed
4. daydreaming
5. free
6. taking
7. easy

Exercise B
a. 3
b. 1
c. 5
d. 2
e. 4

Unit 7
Exercise A
1. party
2. animal
3. lane
4. had
5. up
6. town
7. get
8. owl
9. early

Exercise B
a. 2
b. 1
c. 4
d. 3
e. 5

Unit 8
Exercise A
1. take
2. shotgun
3. gets
4. around/about
5. made
6. take
7. tail
8. in
9. up
10. guzzler

Exercise B
a. 4
b. 3
c. 1
d. 2
e. 5

Unit 9
Exercise A
1. hour
2. drop
3. carpool
4. way
5. buckle
6. off
7. gave
8. share
9. double

Exercise B
a. 4
b. 1
c. 5
d. 2
e. 3

Unit10
Exercise A
1. in
2. rains
3. up
4. off
5. cold
6. cool
7. down
8. up
9. dry

Exercise B
a. 3
b. 1
c. 2
d. 5
e. 4

Review: Units 1–10
Exercise A
1. a
2. c
3. a
4. b
5. a
6. b
7. c
8. c
9. a
10. b

Exercise B
1. T
2. T
3. F
4. T
5. F
6. T
7. T
8. F
9. F
10. T

Exercise C
ACROSS
4. about
6. collar
8. stay
9. animal
10. dishes
DOWN
1. buckle
2. guzzler
3. break
5. around
6. crack
7. rain
8. sleep

Unit 11
Exercise A
1. sight
2. ice
3. Long
4. going
5. seen
6. So
7. small
8. shoot
9. Catch
10. strike
11. hands

Exercise B
a. 2
b. 4
c. 5
d. 1
e. 3

Unit12

Exercise A
1. hook
2. crank
3. hang
4. called
5. phone
6. make
7. on
8. up
9. hold

Exercise B
a. 3
b. 1
c. 4
d. 5
e. 2

Unit 13

Exercise A
1. back
2. touch
3. heard
4. off
5. yackety
6. junk
7. ear
8. mile
9. get
10. line

Exercise B
a. 2
b. 1
c. 3
d. 5
e. 4

Unit 14

Exercise A
1. pop
2. out
3. up
4. books
5. signed
6. drop
7. class(es)
8. in
9. pet

Exercise B
a. 3
b. 1
c. 2
d. 5
e. 4

Unit 15

Exercise A
1. window
2. picks
3. sale
4. hunt
5. up
6. stock
7. take
8. around
9. pick
10. raincheck

Exercise B
a. 1
b. 5
c. 2
d. 4
e. 3

Unit16

Exercise A
1. leftovers
2. out
3. eat
4. junk
5. doggy
6. down
7. pig
8. luck
9. up
10. sweet

Exercise B
a. 2
b. 5
c. 4
d. 3
e. 1

Unit 17

Exercise A
1. settle
2. takes
3. down
4. flesh
5. brought
6. from
7. grew
8. birth

Exercise B
a. 3
b. 5
c. 4
d. 2
e. 1

Unit 18

Exercise A
1. up
2. with
3. blind
4. flame
5. up

6. out
7. with
8. go

Exercise B
a. 2
b. 4
c. 1
d. 3
e. 5

Unit19

Exercise A
1. over
2. asked
3. turned
4. free
5. about
6. along
7. took
8. raincheck

Exercise B
a. 2
b. 5
c. 3
d. 4
e. 1

Unit 20

Exercise A
1. in
2. pay
3. by
4. show
5. home
6. felt
7. together
8. seat
9. stop
10. out

Exercise B
a. 2
b. 5
c. 1
d. 4
e. 3

Review: Units 11–20

Exercise A
1. c
2. a
3. b
4. b
5. a
6. c
7. c
8. a
9. b
10. a

Exercise B
1. F
2. T
3. F
4. T

5. T
6. T
7. F
8. F
9. T
10. F

Exercise C
ACROSS
2. tooth
4. touch
5. dropout
7. yackety
9. brush
11. together
12. books
13. around
DOWN
1. stopover
3. hunter
6. visit
8. about
9. block
10. steady

Unit 21

Exercise A
1. catch
2. up
3. weight
4. work
5. build
6. out
7. diet
8. shape
9. cool
10. lay

Exercise B
a. 4
b. 1
c. 5
d. 3
e. 2

Unit 22

Exercise A
1. running
2. feel
3. around
4. up
5. gets
6. worse
7. checkup
8. course
9. weather
10. down
11. run

Exercise B
a. 1
b. 4
c. 5
d. 2
e. 3

Answer Key

Unit 23

Exercise A
1. go
2. on
3. try
4. dress
5. worn
6. off
7. get
8. out
9. fold
10. bundle

Exercise B
a. 5
b. 3
c. 1
d. 4
e. 2

Unit 24

Exercise A
1. leg
2. rip
3. tab
4. comes
5. without
6. meet
7. broke
8. steal
9. corners
10. get

Exercise B
a. 3
b. 4
c. 5
d. 1
e. 2

Unit 25

Exercise A
1. being
2. later
3. time
4. day
5. now
6. while
7. In/After
8. over
9. for
10. time

Exercise B
a. 2
b. 4
c. 1
d. 5
e. 3

Unit 26

Exercise A
1. by
2. for
3. foot
4. low
5. nose
6. back
7. move
8. up
9. room
10. sit
11. stand

Exercise B
a. 4
b. 1
c. 3
d. 2
e. 5

Unit 27

Exercise A
1. off
2. get
3. off
4. gone
5. off
6. sneak
7. dash
8. out
9. head

Exercise B
a. 5
b. 3
c. 1
d. 4
e. 2

Unit 28

Exercise A
1. down
2. order
3. running
4. up
5. turn
6. up
7. off
8. burned
9. apart

Exercise B
a. 3
b. 4
c. 5
d. 1
e. 2

Unit 29

Exercise A
1. off
2. coming
3. turned
4. sold
5. rains
6. place
7. fell

8. away
9. ring
10. house

Exercise B
a. 2
b. 1
c. 5
d. 3
e. 4

Unit 30

Exercise A
1. part
2. count
3. hand
4. sit
5. out
6. team
7. on
8. show

Exercise B
a. 3
b. 4
c. 1
d. 5
e. 2

Review: Units 21–30

Exercise A
1. c
2. a
3. a
4. b
5. c
6. a
7. c
8. b
9. a
10. b

Exercise B
1. T
2. F
3. T
4. F
5. F
6. T
7. F
8. T
9. F
10. T

Exercise C
Across
5. show
6. broke
8. robbery
9. turnout
10. head
Down
1. later
2. ready

3. room
4. checkup
6. being
7. weather

Unit 31

Exercise A
1. going
2. minded
3. off
4. across
5. know
6. absent
7. getter
8. penny
9. pooper

Exercise B
a. 3
b. 1
c. 4
d. 5
e. 2

Unit 32

Exercise A
1. world
2. ordinary
3. picture
4. date
5. spick
6. dog
7. pits
8. clear
9. rate
10. brand

Exercise B
a. 5
b. 2
c. 1
d. 3
e. 4

Unit 33

Exercise A
1. out
2. alley
3. hand
4. touch
5. thumbs
6. wet
7. knack
8. green
9. hang

Exercise B
a. 3
b. 4
c. 1
d. 2
e. 5

Unit 34
Exercise A
1. finger
2. keep
3. around
4. midnight
5. out
6. feet
7. candle
8. horns
9. half

Exercise B
a. 2
b. 5
c. 3
d. 1
e. 4

Unit 35
Exercise A
1. ups
2. hitch
3. head
4. against
5. straits
6. can
7. piece
8. trouble
9. in
10. brainer

Exercise B
a. 4
b. 1
c. 5
d. 2
e. 3

Unit 36
Exercise A
1. tip
2. mind
3. milk
4. slip
5. forgive
6. back
7. pops
8. faded
9. on
10. heart

Exercise B
a. 5
b. 3
c. 4
d. 2
e. 1

Unit 37
Exercise A
1. come
2. over
3. across
4. up
5. into
6. found
7. after
8. look
9. turned
10. come

Exercise B
a. 3
b. 5
c. 1
d. 2
e. 4

Unit 38
Exercise A
1. message
2. wrong
3. point
4. heads
5. catch
6. ear
7. figure
8. beyond
9. get
10. Greek

Exercise B
a. 2
b. 1
c. 3
d. 5
e. 4

Unit 39
Exercise A
1. fill
2. first
3. break
4. up
5. spread
6. posted
7. catch
8. scoop
9. hot
10. in

Exercise B
a. 5
b. 1
c. 2
d. 4
e. 3

Unit 40
Exercise A
1. ground
2. tangent
3. touch
4. word
5. raise
6. bring
7. go
8. around
9. break
10. speak

Exercise B
a. 2
b. 1
c. 4
d. 3
e. 5

Review: Units 31–40
Exercise A
1. b
2. c
3. a
4. b
5. c
6. a
7. b
8. a
9. c
10. c

Exercise B
1. T
2. T
3. F
4. T
5. F
6. T
7. F
8. T
9. T
10. F

Exercise C
ACROSS
1. thumb
6. world
7. question
8. hitch
10. finger
11. ordinary
12. tail
DOWN
2. mouth
3. nighter
4. find
5. tongue
9. midnight

Unit 41
Exercise A
1. day
2. ear
3. heaven
4. long
5. tear
6. camper
7. smiles
8. blue/down
9. spirits
10. down

Exercise B
a. 3
b. 5
c. 1
d. 2
e. 4

Unit 42
Exercise A
1. voice
2. steam
3. crazy
4. pain
5. short
6. stormed
7. blow
8. hit
9. red
10. off

Exercise B
a. 4
b. 5
c. 1
d. 2
e. 3

Unit 43
Exercise A
1. late
2. with
3. hold/hang
4. out
5. up
6. sat
7. time
8. tied
9. off

Exercise B
a. 4
b. 5
c. 2
d. 1
e. 3

Unit 44
Exercise A
1. none
2. gets
3. busy
4. Knock
5. stick
6. mind
7. away
8. way

Exercise B
a. 2
b. 3
c. 4
d. 5
e. 1

Unit 45

Exercise A

1. better
2. like
3. rather
4. supposed
5. do
6. got
7. dibs
8. much
9. do
10. for

Exercise B

a. 4
b. 3
c. 1
d. 5
e. 2

Unit 46

Exercise A

1. old
2. sleep
3. content
4. kick
5. forward
6. taken
7. into
8. interest
9. took
10. turn

Exercise B

a. 5
b. 1
c. 3
d. 4
e. 2

Unit 47

Exercise A

1. words
2. make
3. benefit
4. word
5. in
6. on
7. sure
8. ands
9. break
10. take

Exercise B

a. 3
b. 1
c. 4
d. 5
e. 2

Unit 48

Exercise A

1. hand
2. ahead
3. head
4. view
5. green
6. favor
7. afraid
8. sounds
9. question
10. dirty

Exercise B

a. 2
b. 3
c. 4
d. 5
e. 1

Unit 49

Exercise A

1. ball
2. level
3. mind
4. keep
5. wits
6. together
7. hold
8. Get

Exercise B

a. 4
b. 1
c. 2
d. 3
e. 5

Unit 50

Exercise A

1. grade
2. ahead
3. square
4. up
5. blew
6. lost
7. vain
8. come
9. big
10. off
11. go

Exercise B

a. 4
b. 3
c. 5
d. 1
e. 2

Review: Units 41–50

Exercise A

1. a
2. b
3. c
4. c
5. a
6. c
7. a
8. b
9. c
10. b

Exercise B

1. T
2. T
3. F
4. T
5. F
6. T
7. T
8. T
9. F
10. F

Exercise C

ACROSS

3. jerker
5. towel
6. business
7. content
10. ahead
11. roof

DOWN

1. matter
2. heaven
4. nothing
6. better
7. crazy
8. Knock
9. hand